I BOUGHT A BOAT (and end(

I BOUGHT A BOAT

(and ended up with 24)

The sequel to 'It's Muck You Want!'

JACK ORRELL
With two chapters by SHEILA ORRELL

To my darling wife Sheila, with love, and thanks for Chapters 8 and 19
which record our sailing trip from Lymington to Beaumaris and our walk
around Anglesey.
J.O.

ISBN
1 901253 53 8
Published July 2006, reprinted March 2010

British Library Cataloguing in Publication Data.
A catalogue record for this book
is available from the British Library

Published by:
Léonie Press
an imprint of
Anne Loader Publications
13 Vale Road, Hartford,
Northwich, Cheshire CW8 1PL Gt Britain
Tel: +44 (0)1606 75660
e-mail: anne@leoniepress.com
Website: www.anneloaderpublications.co.uk
www.leoniepress.com

Printed by:
Poplar Printing Services, St Helens

ABOUT THE AUTHOR

Jack (the name he has been known by since childhood, although he was christened 'John Edward') was born in Walton, Liverpool on June 2nd, 1915. His father, who was a Sergeant in the R.G.A., was killed on the Somme in 1917, so Jack was raised in a household consisting of his mother, her spinster sister, two half sisters, an African green parrot, a Sealyham and two Pekinese dogs. Sometimes the cacophony of confused sound got him down, so he developed a protective 'Deaf Ear' which he sometimes malpractices on his wife, Sheila – much to her annoyance.

He went to Alsops High School in Liverpool and enjoyed a happy but uneventful childhood. Life changed suddenly when his elder sister Eileen married. Her husband, Ron, a 6ft 'he-man', became his hero figure. He taught Jack so much – a knowledge of the countryside, fishing, shooting and a love of motor bikes and then cars.

He trained him in the art of self-defence, and even tried to convince Jack's widowed mother that he had a future as as prize fighter. An uncle thought Jack should follow his example and be a dentist. This was abhorrent to Jack who wished to be a motor mechanic. Eventually a compromise was reached and he became an optician.

The most important thing Ron taught him was that whatever task you set yourself, it should be done to perfection. This is a practice to which he has adhered all his life.

CONTENTS

BEAUFORT SCALE: Specifications and equivalent speeds for use at sea

FORCE	EQUIVALENT SPEED mph	knots	DESCRIPTION	SPECIFICATIONS FOR USE AT SEA
0	0-1	0-1	Calm	Sea like a mirror
1	1-3	1-3	Light air	Ripples with the appearance of scales are formed, but without foam crests.
2	4-7	4-6	Light Breeze	Small wavelets, still short, but more pronounced. Crests have a glassy appearance and do not break.
3	8-12	7-10	Gentle Breeze	Large wavelets. Crests begin to break. Foam of glassy appearance. Perhaps scattered white horses.
4	13-18	11-16	Moderate Breeze	Small waves, becoming larger; fairly frequent white horses.
5	19-24	17-21	Fresh Breeze	Moderate waves, taking a more pronounced long form; many white horses are formed. Chance of some spray.
6	25-31	22-27	Strong Breeze	Large waves begin to form; the white foam crests are more extensive everywhere. Probably some spray.
7	32-38	28-33	Near Gale	Sea heaps up and white foam from breaking waves begins to be blown in streaks along the direction of the wind.
8	39-46	34-40	Gale	Moderately high waves of greater length; edges of crests begin to break into spindrift. The foam is blown in well-marked streaks along the direction of the wind.
9	47-54	41-47	Severe Gale	High waves. Dense streaks of foam along the direction of the wind. Crests of waves begin to topple, tumble and roll over. Spray may affect visibility.
10	55-63	48-55	Storm	Very high waves with long over-hanging crests. The resulting foam, in great patches, is blown in dense white streaks along the direction of the wind. On the whole the surface of the sea takes on a white appearance. The 'tumbling' of the sea becomes heavy and shock-like. Visibility affected.
11	64-72	56-63	Violent Storm	Exceptionally high waves (small and medium-size ships might be for a time lost to view behind the waves). The sea is completely covered with long white patches of foam lying along the direction of the wind. Everywhere the edges of the wave crests are blown into froth. Visibility affected.
12	73-83	64-71	Hurricane	The air is filled with foam and spray. Sea completely white with driving spray; visibility very seriously affected.

Jack, the skipper

BOATS OWNED
WITH CLASS AND NAMES

Snipe: *"Urchin"*
GP 14: *"Tamba"*, *"Tammy"*
Firefly: *"Fleur"*
Mirror: *"Titch"*
Albacore: *"Miranda"*, *"Balarina"*, *"Sunset"*
Flying Dutchman: *"Water Music"*
Liverpool Bay Falcon: *"Golden Eagle"*, *"Levant"*
Squib: *"Tern Turtle"*
1912 Wooden Sloop: *"Florenian"*
Westerly Centaur: *"Emerald Blue"*
Westerly Pageant: *"Magic"*
Contessa 32: *"Coquette"*
Moody 33: *"Magic Dragon"*
Hustler 35: *"Fiddler of Orwell"*
Finsailer 37: *"Jans Fin"*
Catch 22: *"Gambit"*
Seawitch: *"Seawitch"*
Bayliner 22: Cabin Cruiser
Frigate 27: *"Gun Smoke"*
28ft Sloop: *"Sankevic"*

CHAPTER 1

START OF A NEW LIFE

AFTER 10 YEARS spent resurrecting a semi-derelict farm, which is described in my book *It's muck you want!*, my wife Sheila and I finally decided to call it a day in 1961.

For 10 years I had been commuting daily between my two optical practices on the Wirral and our dairy farm in Whixall, Shropshire. It wasn't that I didn't like farming, but the build-up of traffic over the years meant that four hours a day were spent in travelling.

I could of course have sold my optical practices and farmed full-time, but at the time there had been many outbreaks of foot and mouth disease throughout the country and I thought that the possibility of a farming depression was too much of a risk. So we drew a line under our farming adventure, made a clean sweep and started a new life.

One of the things which swung the balance was sailing.

We had started dinghy sailing by going one night a week over to Chester and taking part in the Chester Sailing Club races on the River Dee.

We very soon had the 'sailing bug' and when Sheila went over to West Kirby and came back with details of the different boats which were raced there at the weekends, I decided straight away that it could possibly be a more enjoyable way of ending my days than getting out of bed in the small hours to attend to a calving or pig farrowing. West Kirby was therefore the place for our next move.

We looked at various houses in the area, but eventually were delighted to find Caldy Wood.

It was a four-bedroom detached house situated at the top of a hill in Caldy Village, surrounded by a heath covered in heather. The

1

house itself backed on to the old Caldy Manor Hospital, which had extensive grounds full of silver birch trees. It had only been built five years earlier, so for a start it had full central heating, which we regarded as a terrific luxury – having just endured 10 winters in an old farmhouse in Shropshire, where in the early morning it was impossible to see out of the bedroom window because it was covered in icicles. There were also two luxury bathrooms, a cocktail bar in the hall, and a delightful lounge with a 12ft picture window which looked down into a super garden composed of natural outcrops of sandstone rocks interspersed with hundreds of heathers. The lower level had a small lawn surrounded by rhododendrons and azalea bushes which gave way to small plantation of silver birches. And finally it backed on to the magnificent gardens of Caldy Manor.

Sheila was absolutely thrilled with the place. After the first few weeks' honeymoon period there, we decided that as it was a modern house all our old furniture was incongruous; so we spent days going around Ideal Home-type exhibitions and ordering lots of expensive replacements.

This was a time when everyone decided that they didn't want antiques, so our four-poster beds, grandfather clocks, horse brasses, oak chests and so on were all disposed of for peanuts.

Relieved of all my farming duties, and the 70-mile journey which I used to do every day, I naturally cast around for fresh interests. First of all we agreed that we ought to have a dog. Dachshunds seemed to be the fashionable breed at the moment, so we got 'Flip'.

He was a lovely puppy, and delighted us with how he used to skid across the polished floor on his little legs. He was a real little man, not at all a lap dog; in fact he used to growl if you attempted to pick him up and put him on your knee – although when you looked him in the eye, he would wag his tail and say he didn't really mean it.

The children adored him and thoroughly spoiled him.

On day I said to Sheila, "I wonder if he likes Stilton cheese?" So I taught him to sit up and gave him a small piece of cheese as a

Flying Dutchman, "Water Music".

reward; after that it became a party piece, and towards the end of a meal he used to look so funny, sitting up with his eyes closed and nearly asleep, waiting for his 'tit-bit'.

Whilst we were on the farm we had a caravan on the shores of Lake Bala and used to go over there for alternate weekends – when it wasn't my turn to help with the milking – to sail our Albacore and Flying Dutchman dinghies. Unfortunately, neither of these classes was sailed at West Kirby.

It seemed foolish to continue going all the way to Bala now that we had the sea and also a super marine lake right on our doorstep, so we decided to sell the caravan and the Albacore, and reluctantly resign our membership of the Bala Sailing Club.

The Dutchman *Water Music* was a superb 19-footer, in which the crew sat out on a flying trapeze. It would plane at over 18 knots, and I was most reluctant to sell it.

Anyway we joined the West Kirby sailing club. When their Regatta came along, I was persuaded by Dick Uren to enter it for the Handicap Class. Dick, a member of the famous Uren family, was a superb helmsman and was the leading light in the club. He was

3

dying to get his hands on *Water Music*, so he asked me if I would let him helm it and be his crew. I was over 45 years old at the time, but anyway I agreed and so the Regatta Day arrived.

Dick had been very clever in spotting that it was an open handicap for boats up to 25ft, which meant that each boat had to sail on its individual handicap. Twelve boats entered, all of different classes. We were of course the scratch boat, meaning that we would have to finish far ahead of the rest of the fleet to make up our handicap time.

"Bang!" went the starting gun and we were away. It was a windward start and we were easily the first over the line; when we got to the top end of the lake Dick was whooping with delight, "Just wait until we get around this buoy!"

It so happened that it was blowing about Force 6, which is quite choppy for a dinghy. Immediately I hoisted the 180sq ft spinnaker and slid out on the trapeze, the bow lifted and we were straight on to a screaming plane. The bow wave was so high that I received a terrific buffeting and was half drowned by the time we passed through the starting line for the first time.

The whole performance had to be repeated twice before we got the finishing gun. We came in 20 minutes ahead of our nearest rival and easily made up our handicap time.

There was a large crowd on the finishing line and Dick, being a bit of a showman, couldn't resist it. "Let's go back and give them a bit of a show!" he said, so back and forth we went for two more spectacular planes.

The next day there was a picture of us in the *Liverpool Daily Post* with a large caption: "Planing at 18 knots on The Dee."

It was a pity that there were no other Flying Dutchmen at West Kirby, so I reluctantly decided that I would have to sell *Water Music*; but before I did so, Ted Pollard, my bank manager and bosom pal, begged me to enter for an International Flying Dutchman meeting down at Poole in Dorset and take him along as crew.

CHAPTER 2

FLYING DUTCHMAN

TED NORMALLY SAILED a GP14 and was a good helmsman; the trouble was that he was only 5ft 4ins and lightly built. The ideal crew for a Dutchman is about 6ft 2ins and 16 stone. I pointed this out to Ted, so he said, "I'll crew on the calm days, and my son will crew for you when it's windy." I had my misgivings, but was keen on the idea of a week's sailing, so decided to give it a go.

When we got down to Poole, we found the place alive with all the famous helmsmen from Holland, Germany, France and Italy. *Water Music*, when I bought her from David Court Hampton, had been prepared for the Olympic Games and was a beautifully equipped and prepared boat, but I was somewhat overawed when I saw the competition.

It was quite unbelievable the state of finish on some of the boats, and they all seemed to have brand new sails by the leading American sail makers.

Ted and I settled in to our hotel and awaited the arrival of his son Martin who I had been assured was "great big fellow". He probably appeared so to Ted but he was actually about 5ft 8ins and weighed 10 stone. Oh dear! Certainly not heavy enough to hold a Dutchman level if the wind really piped up. Anyway we were a cheerful trio and after a few beers it didn't seem to matter much, as we had only come down for fun and against such elite competition didn't expect to be in the prize money.

The first day of the races was bright and warm with a gentle breeze, so I decided that Ted could be the trapeze artist for the day. We were to sail a full Olympic circle course. The starting line was about a mile down the coast.

There were a number of luxurious big power cruisers hovering around, their decks resplendent with bikini-clad lovelies. "Can we give you a tow, Flying Dutchman?" they asked. Ted didn't want asking twice – in fact I thought he was going to jump ship.

On the start line the wind began to freshen, and Ted had to get out on the trapeze.

It was a super start, with 21 boats all in line; after five minutes the leading boat decided to tack so immediately all hell was let loose. The Dutchman has an enormous 84sq foot genoa and this makes it very difficult in a closely-packed fleet to see when your nearest rival is about to tack, so when the boat underneath us roared "Starboard!" I had to respond by tacking immediately. Unfortunately Ted wasn't quite quick enough in climbing back in, so for about 10 seconds he got a good dunking. I can still see his face as he disappeared beneath the waves spluttering, "Oh, Jack!" Anyway he became a lot sharper on the following tacks.

The first few tacks after a start are always a bit hectic, but once the fleet sorts itself out things become a bit easier.

Several boats were not quite quick enough in their response, and so were disqualified in the first 10 minutes. It was a good shakedown race and we finished fifteenth.

The next day was a very different matter. It was pouring with rain; a strong Sou'wester was blowing and had whipped up great white horses.

Ted volunteered his "great big son Martin" as crew. Martin was obviously not nearly heavy enough for these conditions, but he was athletic and very keen to go, so off we went.

The boat had four self-bailers and transom flaps and, believe you me, we certainly needed them. The inside of the boat was awash for most of the time, and poor Martin was worn out by the end of the race, as in order to stop us from capsizing he had to stay out on the trapeze for more than two hours.

We had the most terrific exhilarating sail and somehow were one of the few boats not to submerge.

Fibreglass was just starting to take off at the time, and there were two new fibreglass boats in the race; anyway they both capsized and their crews were left sitting on about 2sq ft of boat waiting for the rescue launch. The in-built buoyancy must have been inadequate to cope as eventually both boats sank and I am not sure if they were ever recovered.

We finished 10th which was half way through the fleet, so we were quite chuffed with the result. Martin had proved himself; and as I said to him when we were half-way around, "If we survive this I will never be scared in a boat again."

The remaining three days were not quite so hectic and I managed to take Ted for one more trip.

We weren't in the prize money but ended up ninth overall which I didn't think was too bad considering the tough competition – and we certainly had a great time socially due to the wonderful hospitality of the Poole Sailing Club.

Martin had come down in his own car and he and Ted both had a tight schedule, so at the conclusion of the racing, after they had given me a hand to load the Dutchman onto its trailer, they both beat a hasty retreat back north.

My son Richard was at that time a pupil at Malvern College so I decided to call in on my way home and say "Hello". When I arrived on the front drive Richard was outside with some of his pals and as they gloated over the Dutchman and my gleaming British Racing Green 3.8 Jaguar, he lapped up their sighs of envy...

It was a long drive back to West Kirby, so after a cup of tea and a cake, I gave him a bit of extra pocket money and departed.

Superb and exciting as the Dutchman was, I soon realised that it would have to go.

If we were to take part in any of the weekend races, we would have to sell it and buy one of the three local class boats – a West Kirby Star, a Hilbre or a Liverpool Bay Falcon.

The Star and the Hilbre were both clinker-built boats, whereas the Falcon at that time was of moulded plywood construction, with a lifting rudder and centre plate.

There were no second-hand boats available so we decided to

have one built. The official builder was Allansons of Freckleton, Lancashire.

We had to wait for some time before our boat was ready, so Sheila and I and the rest of the family spent the rest of the season sailing as crew in other members' boats.

The following spring when our lovely new Falcon was ready we named her *Golden Eagle*.

We soon found out that competition in the class was very hot indeed, and no quarter was given. We kept *Golden Eagle* for about seven years and then swapped her for *Levant* which was a particularly nice-looking boat, but one with which nobody so far had ever won a race.

I spent a considerable time in stripping and tuning her and bought a new suit of sails. Suddenly she started to perform and I began to win races.

There was a lot of gamesmanship in the class and several of the top helmsmen were apt to ignore my calls of "Starboard!" which meant that a boat on port should tack and allow the starboard boat

Racing "Golden Eagle", our 20ft Liverpool Bay Falcon.

right of way. I became frustrated at this attempt at intimidation, so one day held my course and only just missed driving a large hole right in the middle of my opponent's boat; after that word must have got around and I had no further trouble.

The Falcon sailed with a crew of three or four. With her centre-plate lifted and a real blow she could be coaxed on to an exhilarating plane.

Sheila was my regular crew and I'm sure she enjoyed the excitement of racing. Richard, Anne and Jane, our three children, were also eager participants during the school holidays.

Ron and Linda Wilson were the other semi-regulars for a few years and put up with my bullying without complaint.

I can remember one occasion, when we were in the lead and close to the finishing line, that Linda's feet slipped out of the toe-straps when she was leaning out and she disappeared over the side. I just managed to grab her left ankle and I towed her over the line with her head in the water. We won the race. She was a good sport and of course realised that if I had let her go we would have been disqualified, as you have to end up with the crew you started with.

One particular aspect I enjoyed was team racing. Hoylake Sailing Club, which was only two or three miles along the coast, also had a fleet of Falcons, so if you were picked for the West Kirby team you went down to Hoylake, usually on a Friday evening, and together with other members manned usually three of their boats and raced against three boats crewed by Hoylake members. It was great fun and when the racing finished we were invited into their club for supper and liquid refreshment. Ah! No breathalysers or overcrowded roads in those happy days

I raced a Liverpool Bay Falcon for about 10 years. In our final year we ended the season by winning 'Fred', a Falcon replica which is awarded each year for the boat gaining the largest number of points during the Menai Straits Fortnight regatta. We also won six other trophies over the season.

Having achieved my ambition, I handed *Levant* over to Richard and he won many races with her. Alas, she has finally succumbed to the ravages of old age and is no more.

By this time I also had passed the first flush of youth and began to think that it was time we had something bigger.

There were quite a large number of offshore cruisers in the club, and one day I noticed that there was a particularly interesting boat advertised for sale on the club notice board. She belonged to Jamie Hartley, who also raced a Hilbre. *Florenian* was a 30ft carvel-built wooden boat of 1912 vintage. She had originally been gaff rigged and had a bowsprit, but her previous owner, who worked at Cammell Lairds, the famous Birkenhead shipbuilders, had added 2ft on to the stern, done away with the bowsprit and turned her into a sloop. She had a very small fixed keel and a very heavy iron centre plate which was controlled by a rope and pulley system.

By this time Richard had been to London University and qualified as an optometrist. He had a pal, John Jones, who was a dental surgeon; they both liked the idea of having a share in an offshore yacht, so I went into partnership with them, and we bought *Florenian*.

We had her brought into the yard at the West Kirby Sailing Club and spent the entire winter stripping her down to the bare wood and doing a complete re-fit.

There is a famous yearly midnight race from Rock Ferry to Douglas on the Isle of Man. We decided to enter for the event; unfortunately none of us had as yet taken a navigation course, so we took along another club member, David Coulthard, who said he could navigate.

In our rush to get the boat ready for the race, we had not had time to rig up any permanent navigation lights, so we just had to make do with battery torches covered in red and green socks.

The weather forecast had not been very encouraging, with Force 4-5 and possibly 6 on the cards; anyway she appeared to be a stoutly-built boat, so we decided to give it a go.

The start was from the Royal Mersey Yacht club at Rock Ferry.

We had a reasonably gentle wind until we passed The Bar and

it started to get dark. The wind then started to pipe up and we decided to put a reef in the mainsail.

After we had been sailing for about three hours David decided that we ought to put in a tack.

Oh dear!

"What's that?"

There was all of a sudden a tremendous swooching sound. We hadn't realised until then that *Florenian* had taken on a considerable amount of water in her bilge, and it was that which was making the noise. I know now that when a wooden boat has been out of the water for several months the wood shrinks and it takes a few days for it to swell and make her watertight once again, but in those days we had still got a lot to learn...

It was a case of all hands to the pumps but after a while it became obvious that more drastic action was necessary.

By this time John had become the colour of putty, and was being violently seasick. Richard was on the helm, so David and I went below and set to work with relays of buckets. By this time the wind had really increased, and we were reefed right down. We were being hurled about by enormous rollers when suddenly David lost his balance and was hurled head first across the bilge: he hit his head on the corner of one of the drawers and immediately started to pour blood into the water.

We laid him down on one of the bunks which was already awash, and with the aid of a torch investigated the damage. Fortunately it was a piece of skin which had been ripped back, so we did our best to staunch the flow and covered his head in an enormous bandage.

Whoops... he was our navigator !

Richard and I are never seasick, so at least we had a skeleton crew. David slowly recovered sufficiently to tell us when to tack. It all seemed a bit of guesswork and when dawn came we were quite expecting that we had probably missed the Isle of Man altogether. However we were in luck and as the mist began to clear we began to make out a vague outline of land on the horizon.

As we sailed closer inland, the wind dropped dramatically until we were soon becalmed and also had the tide starting to turn against us. We couldn't see any other boats in sight, so we thought that they must have all made the tide before it turned and were already ashore enjoying the 'fleshpots'.

We had a conference, deciding that in view of David's injury and the fact that we had all got to be back at work on Monday morning, it would probably be best to abandon the race, try and start our poor little half-drowned Stuart Turner engine (which was situated in the open cockpit) and wend our way back home.

Once on the way home it wasn't long before we met *Shiloh*, a very smart Sparkman and Stephens 30-footer, heading for the Isle of Man. Guess what? She turned out to be the leading boat and won the race!

It had been one hell of a night with many casualties and retirements, so we weren't too disappointed seeing that it was our first effort.

In spite of her age *Florenian* was a very fast boat and several years before with her previous owner had won the Midnight Race. She was an ideal boat to have as a first cruiser in order to gain experience, because she was completely basic, was practically engineless, had no depth sounder other than a lead line, and only elementary navigational equipment: so that if you were not alert and landed on a sandbank, you stayed there until the tide turned.

We had great fun with her and learned a lot, but after several years the partnership was dissolved.

I still have her old 1912 brass compass, which was illuminated by a little oil lamp, and many fond memories.

Sheila is a qualified optometrist and during the war years when I was abroad in the army she successfully ran our optical practice. On my return she decided that she had had enough and so took a well-deserved break to concentrate on looking after the wellbeing of the family. It was comforting, however, to know that she was always ready to fill in, in an emergency

When Richard qualified, he wanted to join my practice but I advised him that it would probably be better to get a job with someone else in order to gain experience. So he started to work for Jack Hayes in Upton. He was very happy there and Jack even offered him a partnership.

After a year and a half, he decided that he would prefer to join my firm, so Sheila and I offered him a joint partnership. At this time Bill Wilson was also working for me, so when a practice in New Brighton came up for sale I decided to buy it. I also bought the premises. The previous owner had reached retirement age and had tended to take things easy, so the practice required a lot of building up.

I had spent many happy hours in New Brighton as a child; those were the days when we lived in Liverpool, and of course it was a great treat to sail over there on the *Royal Daffodil* to spend the day on the beach and in the paddling pool. At that time it was like a miniature Blackpool with fairgrounds dominating the promenade and a lot of cheap amusement arcades and fish and chip saloons. It had changed a lot over the years and was now showing signs of a new respectability.

In 2005, New Brighton is now a delightful riverside resort with beautifully laid-out streets, squares filled with flowers and rows of attractive town houses. My vision has been rewarded. The practice has now been completely refurbished with all the very latest instrumentation and is run very successfully by Richard.

CHAPTER 3

THE OLD BARRACKS

NEXT DOOR TO our Ellesmere Port practice there was a Medical Centre which was manned by four doctors. One day Kirk Radcliffe, one of the doctors, came in for an eye examination. In the course of conversation he asked if I knew of anyone who wanted to buy a cottage in Anglesey.

At that time Sheila and I used to take our Liverpool Bay Falcon down there for the yearly Straits Regatta, so I asked him for particulars and said that I might possibly be interested.

The next day was a Saturday, and our daughter Jane was with us, so I suggested we should go down and have a look. The address was given as 'The Old Barracks Cottage, Rosemary Lane'.

We picked up the key from Nancy Lomax, a relative of Kirk's who lived in the district, and sallied forth to investigate.

The price which I understood Kirk wanted had conjured up visions of a one-up one-down Welsh cottage. When we got to the entrance there was an enormous big black gate with a small entrance door let into it; we went through into a cobbled courtyard in which there were three attractive flats and on the left side of the yard there was a pathway of rising steps which we ascended. At the top was a super stone-built cottage surrounded by a small but attractive garden.

Something was wrong here! No way was this beautiful place for sale at the price I had thought Kirk had mentioned. It dawned on me that the figure must have had another '0' on it.

We went to the front door, which was of multi-paned glass, and proceeded inside.

There was a hallway, which led off to a small kitchen and a

downstairs bathroom. The winning feature was the lounge, which occupied practically the whole of the ground floor. It was a most attractive room with a glass door and two large windows. There was a very large inglenook-type grate and an oak beamed ceiling.

Upstairs there were three good-sized bedrooms, the walls of which had incorporated in them the ribs of an old sailing ship.

Jane was absolutely thrilled with the place. "Buy it, Dad, buy it!" she begged.

It was all very well, but as I said, I had mistaken the price and had had no intention of buying anything other than a very small holiday cottage.

When we got home we discussed it all evening and tried to think of excuses for buying it. I lay awake for half the night and in the morning I had made up my mind,

If I bought it, we could use it as a weekend retreat; we wouldn't have to pay for holiday accommodation in the future and – yes – it would be an ideal retirement home that would probably appreciate in value in the future. I went to see Kirk and bought it.

In the past the cottage had been the Barracks Hospital and the flats had been the Armoury. The whole complex had been neglected and fallen into ruins before Kirk bought it. He had engaged the services of local stonemasons Ken Thomas and his father to carry out a complete restoration, so it had a new roof of Welsh slate and was in perfect condition when we took over.

All the family were delighted, and were soon queuing up for free seaside holidays. So began our love affair with Anglesey. Let me tell you some more about it:

MON CYMRU (mother of Wales)

When you cross the lovely old suspension bridge, constructed by Thomas Telford you are entering the magical island of Anglesey. Before the arrival of the bridge this was the spot where at low tide cattle for sale had to swim across to the mainland.

Anglesey has a more equable climate than the mainland, and has a wondrous coastline teeming with wildlife.

15

A mile along the coast from our present cottage, Minnows, is Puffin Island and Lighthouse, As the name would suggest this is the home for the delightful little birds which inhabit it. Sad to say over the years due to the hundreds of rats on the island who fed on their eggs the stock of birds has been seriously depleted. Five years ago a determined rat extermination programme was carried out, and now numbers are slowly on the increase.

During the warmer months daily boat excursions are made to the island by the many visitors anxious to see its thriving seal colony.

Puffin is the gateway to the Menai Straits, the constantly-changing strip of water which separates us from the mainland.

From our conservatory we have a wonderful view of the multitude of birds which migrate up and down with the flow of the tide; oystercatchers in their hundreds, soaring and diving in the air currents, shelduck with their gorgeous black, white and chestnut plumage, arctic terns diving for their dinner, great crested grebes, golden eye, and of course the beady eyed herons which periodically attempt to raid my fish pond..

Sheila and I decided that to really appreciate our lovely island the only way was to circumnavigate it on foot. This we did, and on our return Sheila was so impressed that she sat down a week after we returned and wrote an account of our exploits.

I cannot attempt to remember more than 30 years later all the details of the walk so I will let her tell you in her own words, which she will do in Chapter 19.

CHAPTER 4

CALDY WOOD

CALDY WOOD, our West Kirby home, was a dream house and Sheila absolutely loved it, but after four years I began to have certain misgivings. The main snag for me was that it was usually 6:30pm when I arrived home, and after my evening meal I liked to go outside and do a bit of gardening. I wasn't the only one who liked to be outside. Due to the proximity of dozens of lovely silver birch trees, all the mosquitoes for miles around used to meet up for a nightly party – and I was the favourite dish. After half an hour I was usually glad to crawl back inside.

One day I heard that there was a house for sale on the promenade; it belonged to a friend of Sheila's, Edna Crossley, whose husband Roy had recently had a heart attack. The house had a large garden with 500 rose bushes, and was perched high above the promenade. Roy's doctor had told him that under no circumstances must he continue to climb up the steep path or attempt the steps up to the house.

I was on my way to my practice, and so had only got 15 minutes to spare, but decided to stop and investigate. There was a car outside and an attractive dark-haired lady was busy loading it with bits of household goods. There was no 'For Sale' notice up.

I approached her, saying, "Good morning, I believe the house is for sale?"

She replied, "Yes, it is, but my father has taken it off the market for the present as he wants to have a bit of redecorating done."

"May I have a quick look?"

"Well, it will have to be quick, because I have got an appointment to keep."

17

I went up the steps, and scampered from room to room.

It was an older house, and slightly larger than Caldy Wood. The lounge had a large double-glazed window, which looked out on to a rock garden, with the promenade and marine lake in the background. There were four bedrooms; but what I really fell for was the master bedroom, which had its own dressing room and private bathroom. There were two windows, the side window overlooked a large private hotel called Redcote, and the front one, which was the full width of the room, had a bird's eye view of the whole of the Dee estuary.

The position was superb, and what is more, there was a back entrance through the rose garden on to the main shopping road.

I felt that I would really kick myself if I missed this gem. I could already picture myself sitting out on the front veranda of an evening (minus mosquitoes), and with a drink in my hand watching the dinghy racing.

I was running late for my appointments, and I didn't want any hitch up, so I just said. "Right! You've got a sale!"

Hilary, who turned out to be Roy's daughter, was gobsmacked. Anyway I gave her my solicitor's phone number and told her to get in touch with him.

When I got home that evening I quietly said to Sheila, "Do you like that house of Edna's?"

"Yes," she replied. "It's got a lovely view, and it's very convenient for the shops."

"I'm glad you like it, because I've just bought it…"

There was a bit of recrimination, because Sheila was so fond of Caldy Wood and of course the 'mossies' were not there in the daytime when she could sit out in the garden. Anyway she soon saw the advantage of being able to walk to the shops and the sailing club – and she certainly fell for the early morning view from our super bedroom suite.

It turned out that Roy and Edna were in Spain at the time. Roy had been a fruit and onion importer, and spoke fluent Spanish. They were a lovely devoted couple, and when Roy died several generations of his Spanish friends were present at the funeral.

Edna is now over 90 years of age and is living in a retirement home in West Kirby.

When we settled down at "Spindrift" Sheila found that she had lots of spare time, so she joined the Wirral Ladies Golf Club. She would really have liked to be a member of Caldy Golf Club but there was a rule that a lady could only join if her husband was already a member.

It was a small and very elite club and I was encouraged to apply for membership. There was a long waiting list and when my turn came I had to appear before the committee, together with my sponsor, for interrogation. It was quite a searching probe and included such questions as "How long have you lived in the district?", "Where were you educated?", "What is your profession?" and "Have you any other hobbies?" The final question was "If there was a golf match and a sailing regatta on the same day, which would you attend?" I crossed my fingers and gave the obvious answer.

In a week's time I got a letter welcoming me to membership. In due course Sheila became a lady member, and thoroughly enjoyed entering for the weekly competitions.

Sailing, of course, was my premier love, so I am afraid I didn't make as much use of the golf club as she did.

CHAPTER 5

SEARCH FOR A NEW BOAT

HAVING DISSOLVED the *Florenian* partnership, and now having an additional delightful cottage in Anglesey, we thought that we should look out for a modern, more easily-managed cruiser – something that didn't demand a crew of trained gorillas.

We joined the North West Venturers Sailing Club, the clubhouse of which is situated at Gallows Point, Beaumaris.

We sought the advice of various club members as to the best type of yacht for cruising around the Island. They all stressed the advantages of a twin-keel vessel for taking the ground in all the little bays around Anglesey. The only snag is that a twin-keeler is not generally as fast as a single-keeler and won't point as high.

We decided to visit Dickies Boat Yard and ask the advice of Peter Dickie, the managing director. He said he thought he had just the boat for us.

It turned out to be a year-old Westerly Centaur twin-keeler. He assured us that they were very seaworthy boats which had even crossed oceans and that it also had the advantage of an almost new Volvo twin inboard engine.

Emerald Blue, as she was called, had dark blue topsides, and seemed to be in nearly-new condition. She was 30ft long, had four berths and full 6ft 4ins headroom throughout her cabins.

She was of course constructed of fibreglass, so would not have all the problems of "old Flo". We decided to buy. She proved to be an excellent choice as a cruiser for two relatively inexperienced middle-aged people.

To start with, before we did any long-distance cruising, we went on several weekend trips with other members of the club. There are a number of favourite anchorages around the Island, such as Moelfre, Pilots Cove, Newborough and Porth Dinllyn. The advantage of going with the 'old hands' of course

We were really enjoying our cruising adventures

was that they knew the best spots to anchor – they even took us on one occasion right inside The Skerries to deliver a loaf of bread to the lighthouse keeper.

Once you had made sure that your anchor was holding and the evening meal was over, the ritual was to man your rubber dinghy and join up with the others on whichever boat was having a party; or if we were on an anchorage where there was a pub we would all meet up there.

If we were going to cruise further afield the next step was to fit the boat out with basic navigation equipment, and learn to navigate.

I sent away for a correspondence course on navigation and seamanship, and we also attended a weekend course on navigation at Burton Manor.

If you want to cruise off shore you can't just sail by 'the seat of your pants', you've got to learn all about mean tides, dead reckoning (I didn't like the sound of that), cocked hats, depth sounders, electronic position finders and all the intricacies of a ship-to-shore radio, so that you can communicate with the coastguard and other ships and if necessary send out an SOS or a PAM PAM.

Before you can operate the radio you have to take an exam, obtain a certificate of proficiency and have the set licensed.

Every year in August the Venturers take a three-week cruise up to Scotland. They reckon on a week to get up there, a week spent cruising all the different lochs and places of interest, and a week to sail back home. Having mastered the rudiments of navigation and the intricacies of 'rafting up' and tying up in harbours, we decided that we would join them and hope that we wouldn't disgrace ourselves.

The Venturers were a great crowd and we felt that if we got in any difficulties we would get a helping hand.

There were usually about nine boats which made the cruise together, and they ranged in size from Gordon and Marjorie Rutter's *Seamint* which was a 35ft ketch, to George Driver's 27ft sloop *Trisala* which he sailed single-handed.

Gordon and Marjorie were really the guiding lights of the club, as they had in their early sailing days trailed a large dinghy up to Scotland, and had for many years sailed into practically every loch and harbour on the way.

CHAPTER 6

OUR FIRST CRUISE

ON THIS OUR first real cruise in *Emerald Blue*, unfortunately, due to staff difficulties, I could only afford to be two weeks away from home, which would not be long enough to do the full Scottish cruise with the club.

We decided that when they started off we would tag along with them for the first few ports of call to get a bit of help and experience, and then return home to Beaumaris on our own.

The great day arrived; at 7:00am we cast off our mooring and together with eight other boats set forth for Port St Mary, on the Isle of Man. It turned out to be quite a calm sea, with about a Force 3, so it was quite a gentle 'shake down'.

Before we reached harbour we dropped our sails, started our faithful Volvo and motored in. It's always a bit worrying entering harbour and wondering where to moor.

The harbour was occupied by a fleet of fishing boats, so there wasn't much room. *Seamint*, which was just ahead of us, motored across to one of the smaller vessels and tied up alongside. Sheila hung four of our large fenders on the port side and we decided to moor up next to *Seamint*.

Mooring in a crowded harbour is quite a complicated business and entails juggling a lot of rope. First of all you have to put on 'springs' – this consists of a line from your bow to the stern of your neighbour, and then a line from your stern to your neighbour's bow. It is then necessary to take fore and aft lines over all your neighbours right up to the harbour wall. If the harbour is crowded this can involve clambering over seven boats, then climbing up a vertical ladder which is attached to the harbour wall and making

Safe arrival in the IoM.

the ropes fast (not to be recommended in the dark if it's pouring with rain).

We had a day of rest in Port St Mary, and did a tour of the island before joining some of the other crews for a meal at the Bay View Hotel. Their fresh crab was delicious.

The next leg of the cruise was up to Port Patrick. This is always a popular place as it is a very well-sheltered harbour and there is also a super little pub right on the quayside, which is famous for its steaks, and scampi and chips. There is a small pottery, so if one stops in on the way home it's useful for purchasing small gifts.

Girvan was our next stop, and we tied up alongside the pier. The old hands said that there was a smashing indoor swimming pool here, so we rooted out our swimming costumes and joined in the fun. They also had excellent hot baths, so after our swim we indulged in a good soak.

We were beginning to relax, and were enjoying every minute of our cruising; unfortunately the weather was beginning to deteriorate and a Force 5-6 wind was forecast. Early the next day the fleet decided to make a dash for Campbeltown – a nice little fishing port and shopping centre for the area. We had a reasonable passage over there and tied up alongside the pier.

By late afternoon a heavy swell started to come in to the harbour; that was just the beginning. By midnight all hell was let loose. The whole of the landing stage was awash; the wind shrieked and howled in the rigging and at times we were almost being lifted clean out of the water. Fortunately I had a large barge board with me and I jammed this between the row of fenders and the stone of the pier. It was a job to try and keep it down and I had no option but to dash on deck every 15 minutes and re-set it. It was impossible to keep dry so I didn't bother to put any clothes on, and just towelled myself down when I went below. Next morning the storm abated somewhat, but it was two more days before it was fit to leave the harbour.

We had heard from various sources that half a mile across the causeway there was a small island on which there was a cave with a painting of Christ on one of its walls. Although the weather was atrocious, Philip Robinson, one of our crewmates, and I used one of our enforced delay days to investigate.

It really was tough struggling around the seaweed-covered slimy rocks in a howling gale, but when we reached the cave and entered

Rafting up in Port Patrick.

25

we were bewitched by a magnificent life-size painting of Christ. It had apparently been done some years ago by an artist who had discovered the cave and had felt the need to express himself. Over the years some of the colours had faded but apparently the artist was still alive and I believe that some years later he returned to restore it to its former glory.

In view of our restricted time and the possibility of encountering further storms, we decided that we had better wave goodbye to the rest of the fleet, who were still heading further north up to Scotland, and re-trace our lonely way back to Beaumaris.

We were lucky and had a good steady Force 3 to 4 reaching wind all the way to the Isle of Man. We had two days in hand so stayed in the harbour there and relaxed. On our final leg home the wind died and we had to motor most of the way.

We felt that our first cruise had been a great success and were eagerly looking forward to the next time.

CHAPTER 7

FAREWELL TO 'SPINDRIFT'

WHEN OUR SON Richard joined us in the practice, my assistant Bill Wilson, who had been working for me for a number of years, started to get itchy feet. Bill and I had worked very well together, and I would have liked to have offered him a partnership, but Richard didn't feel that the time was right to take in an additional partner.

I was 65 and contemplating retirement, so reluctantly I had to accept Bill's decision to move on to pastures new.

We needed help to cope with our bulging appointment list so we decided to take on a Pre Registration Optician – one who has qualified but has to spend a year in an established practice, under supervision, before acquiring registration.

We had a number of applications, but the best of the bunch was John Bennett.

John was obviously the product of wealthy parents as he arrived in a brand new bright red MGB.GT. He was a bright and cheerful pupil, and was eager and willing to perform any task he was given. At the end of his year I was happy to sign the necessary papers condoning his ability. I would have been more than happy to have retained his services, but he wished to start a practice of his own.

We had now been at "Spindrift" for a number of years, and it was delightful to be able to sit out on the terrace on a summer's evening, looking down onto the marine lake where there was always something interesting to watch.

Unfortunately, all good things have to come to an end, and our halcyon days ended when the large Redcote Hotel next door was put up for sale. We waited with bated breath to see who the new owner would be. We didn't have long to wait.

Oh dear! It had been bought by a well-known local property developer, so we realised that it wouldn't be long before it would be demolished and a block of flats erected in its place.

Three months later, all hell was let loose. A demolition team arrived with a couple of JCB tractors and proceeded to tear the place apart. Our peaceful days had ended.

From 8:00 in the morning until 5:30 in the afternoon we were subjected to the sound of falling masonry, clouds of dust, burst water mains, and at night showers of electric sparks from where they had severed cables.

I think that they were purposely making our lives as miserable as they possibly could, as one day I received a phone call from the manager of one of the local estate agents asking if he could come to see me as he had a very attractive offer to put to me if we would consider selling our house.

I had been very happy before the maelstrom next door started and had not contemplated a removal, however I could see that if we stayed we would be subjected to months of frustration, and would finally end up with a high-rise block of flats next door, which would partially restrict our wonderful view down the marine lake. There was also an other consideration to think of; I was now 65 and was thinking of retiring in a year's time, and we had been considering the idea of a possible move down to our delightful cottage in Beaumaris.

The agent duly arrived, and his offer of approximately twice the market value of our house was indeed tempting. We mulled it over and decided that we would accept the offer, and leave all the chaos behind us.

Richard was now working in the practices, but did not feel quite ready to take full charge if I retired immediately.

We decided that our ultimate aim would be to retire to Anglesey in about a year's time; so we had to start looking for alternative accommodation. Fortunately a one-bedroom flat on the promenade at Hoylake had just come on the market, so we went to inspect it.

It was a cheerful little flat with a decent-sized lounge and adequate bedroom. The kitchen was a little sparse but it had a nice new shower room. It also had gas central heating which had just been installed. "Great!" we thought. It was just what we needed, so we bought it.

The idea now was that we would retire to Anglesey, and return to stay in Hoylake for four days a fortnight for a year, so that I could gradually hand over the practices.

This was fine in theory, but I didn't look forward to my four-day stint, as of course all the really difficult and awkward patients were usually 'saved' for me to sort out, and I was always booked solid from 9:00am to 6:00pm. I usually worked Tuesday, Wednesday, Thursday and Friday, and sure was glad to clamber into my Jaguar for the long drive to Anglesey on a Friday evening.

When the final day came for the completion of the sale of "Spindrift", the agent rang to say that there was a snag in that they were £5000 short of the agreed price, and were not able to complete. This was obviously a "try on" and we were very angry; but by this time we were mentally and physically drained, so we accepted the lesser sum.

We decided that if they could play games, so could we. So before we vacated I arranged for a plumber to disconnect all the stainless steel kitchen units and transfer them to the Hoylake flat.

We received a solicitor's letter from the builders asking for their return. I just ignored it.

With a nice tidy sum now in the bank I decided to buy a car I had always wanted, a 280 SL Mercedes Coupe. We then booked in for a week's rest at the Clifton Hotel in Bournemouth.

At the time it was the only 5-star privately owned hotel in Europe, and was a gourmet's retreat. We had a lovely suite on the sea front, with a cocktail cabinet by the side of the king-sized bed. Each day we had gorgeous five-course lunches and seven-course dinners. The waiters were all of the old family retainer type and willingly gave their advice on the merits of all the special dishes we were offered.

With such a choice, we couldn't help over-indulging, and had to go for long walks every day to keep the flab down.

One day we went for a walk in the New Forest. The weather had not been too kind and the ground was somewhat waterlogged; Sheila unfortunately stepped in to a swampy area, and went up to her knees in bright yellow mud.

When we got back to our posh hotel it was afternoon tea-time and all the residents were seated at little lace-covered tables, partaking of cucumber sandwiches and strawberry tartlets. It was the only way in, so my poor embarrassed and mud-plastered wife had to run the gauntlet through to the lift which took us up to our bedroom.

When I retired at the age of 66 we had no further use for our little Hoylake flat so we sold it and distributed most of the contents between Richard and Jane. The one exception was a very luxurious three-piece lounge suite, the settee of which was so large that we had had to take the front window out to get it in. As we couldn't be bothered to get it out, we offered it to the new owners at a knock-

"Coquette" in course of construction at Lymington.

down price.

We had now enjoyed a couple of years cruising in our twin keeler *Emerald Blue*. She was an excellent boat in which to start cruising, but as we became more experienced we began to yearn for something a bit more sporting, which we could enter for the occasional race.

We had been particularly impressed by the gorgeous lines of a boat called a "Contessa". She was 32ft long and a single-keeler. The class was very popular at the time and there were very few decent specimens about, so we decided to order a new one, which we called *Coquette*. There was a long waiting list for delivery, and it was nearly a year before we got word that our boat was nearly ready. She was built at Jeremy Roger's yard at Lymington so was duly launched and commissioned there. A month after our delivery cruise Sheila sat down and wrote an excellent day-to-day account of how we sailed her back to Anglesey, so I'm now going to hand you over to her...

CHAPTER 8

TURN RIGHT AT LAND'S END

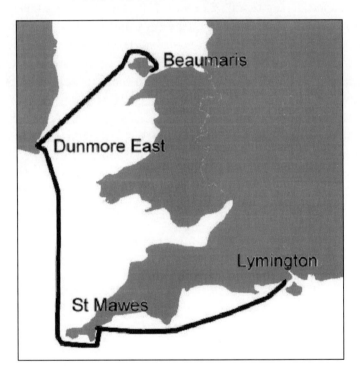

THIS IS THE account of the maiden voyage of *Coquette*, a beautiful Contessa 32 class boat, from Lymington to Anglesey, *writes Sheila*.

When she was ordered, the question of delivery naturally arose. Fresh from the Southampton Boat Show, it seemed a simple matter to sail her round ourselves, and we arranged to take delivery in early May. Although we have been afloat for many years, it is only recently that we have taken to cruising, as opposed to club racing.

Our previous boat was a bilge-keeler which was very comfortable, and given the right conditions would sail quite fast; however, once bitten by the racing bug, the desire for further speed is fairly strong, and in choosing the Contessa Jack felt that in between cruising we could enter the odd local regatta with a chance of winning.

During the long winter wait for our new boat, the question of crew was discussed. Our ability to navigate had been put to the test but little, as apart from an odd trip to Ireland and the Isle of Man, our experience was limited. Obviously an experienced navigator for a complicated voyage would be a great comfort.

As the Skipper's wife, I was flattered to be given the first invitation, and although I knew I hadn't been asked on account of my navigational skills, I accepted. My chief assets are that I can cook, find things that are lost and I am not seasick.

The next member of the crew was our son Richard. He was not actually asked – he didn't give us time – but said that he was coming and had already made the necessary arrangements to be on holiday at that time. We were more than pleased as he is a very competent seaman and is mad keen on all aspects of navigation; Anne his wife decided not to come on this trip as she is unhappily a poor sailer, at least in a cruising boat. She is however able to enjoy dinghy racing, and I know that with her Yorkshire grit she will have another crack at cruising nearer home.

Philip Robinson was the next choice, as in a rash moment after sailing in a race with us last year, he promised to help us get the new boat home; true to his word he did just that and could both navigate and operate the R.T. set. We rather naively thought that a complement of six would be ideal for a fast passage as we could split into three watches and our spells below would be worthwhile. I had the unworthy thought that the galley work could be shared. On this basis we required two more people. We felt that, given favourable conditions, the trip could be done in four days, but with adverse weather, it could conceivably take a couple of weeks. It is not easy to find experienced people at this time of the year who are prepared to leave jobs and/or wives for an indefinite period and at an indefinite time. Mind you, put out an SOS for crews at one's local sailing club and I suspect that jobs and/or wives would fade into the background.

However, we didn't want to be too unpopular and we did want to be organised. Our final choice was Tony, a friend of ours who is a mechanical wizard, and Phil, a friend of Richard's. He is super-keen, agile as a cat and always good-tempered.

We extracted a promise from him that as the only smoker on board, he would not indulge in his vice in the cabin. It is worthy of note that, half-way home, Phil threw his last cigarette overboard with a grand gesture and took a vow never to smoke again. We were all pretty impressed and still are, even though we have heard that Phil's halo has tarnished just a bit.

After some delays, our boat was to be ready for us on May 15th.

It was decided that Richard and Phil would arrive on Friday night, May 20th, ready for departure on May 21st. On the 15th, Jack, Tony and I travelled down in Tony's campervan, whilst Philip and his wife, Margery arrived in theirs. The plan was to load up the stores, make any necessary adjustments and additions and to have the rest of the week to take the boat out on trials. In fact we were going to enjoy ourselves. Strangely enough we did just that, but not in the least as planned.

The weather was not kind. Every day was cold and windy, with winds Force 6 to 7 and gales forecast in Wight, Portland etc. Not ideal conditions to try out a new boat. The boat itself caused us some problems, and was in fact not entirely ready for occupation.

We had relays of experts coming on board and gradually all our problems were sorted out very cheerfully. By Friday we were able to go down the river on the engine (the sails still had not arrived). It was rough when we got outside. The engine behaved perfectly, but the log – which was not the one that we had ordered – was completely illogical.

We had another 'expert' to try and sort this out, but to no avail. We had already spent some time trying to calibrate the wretched thing ourselves. No further experts were available on Saturday morning, naturally, and we had to face the prospect of a 400-odd mile journey without the use of a log. A challenge indeed to our navigators.

By Saturday we had to decide if and when to leave. Richard and Phil had arrived, Anne had very kindly brought a couple of cooked chickens, some *pâté* and cakes. Margery had departed and we felt sorry that she had not had the sail that she had expected, but that's sailing anyway. Tony had also left for home, due to urgent business matters. He had thought to do the first leg of the trip with us in any case, but the difficulties of getting public transport back to Lymington, plus the by now obvious discomforts to be encountered if six people were sleeping on board, decided him to leave by road and delay his sail with us to a less crowded occasion. He had done so much work around the boat that we felt particularly sorry that he did not get his 'reward'. The wind remained much the same, north-easterly. Philip thought that we should leave on the Saturday as the wind was in our favour and conditions in the Irish Sea were delightful and might very well worsen by the time we got there if we delayed too long. We were of mixed opinions about this as we had as yet not tried the sails. We were advised by a kindly neighbour on the marina to leave our departure until we had at least had a sail. This we did and were rather glad about. The boat was a delight and we had a pretty rough sail, admittedly having to come on the wind in order to return to Lymington. We decided to leave on the Sunday at mid-day with the tide.

Our stay on the marina had been quite pleasant and we certainly enjoyed the near luxury of hot showers, etc. We had met quite a few people including a charming Dutch family who had just taken delivery of their Contessa and who were going to sail her back to Holland later in the week.

We thought of the comfortable marina that we would leave. There were no 'facilities' where we were going.

Merely to get on and off our boats can be quite hazardous at times, but hazardous as may be, the Menai Straits are indeed beautiful.

Perhaps we were getting homesick.

Tomorrow we would leave.

As intended, we left Lymington at 12 noon on the Sunday.

North-easterly 5-6 was forecast, locally Force 7. We thought that we would make for Falmouth on the first leg of the journey, but were prepared if necessary to put into Dartmouth. It was a lovely day with blue skies and wisps of fine white cloud. It was cold, of course, and the wind continued nicely behind us down the channel. The seas were quite big. None of us had seen the channel, at least from a yacht, and we had been warned of the uncomfortable motion to be felt.

As we headed for the Needles channel we felt good.

The Needles themselves looked good, shining white under a clear blue sky. Cameras came out and a few pleasant pictures were taken. We became aware that the wind had moderated and decided that the time had come to try out our lovely red, white and blue spinnaker.

What a confusion of sheets and guys – far more complicated than anything that we had dealt with previously. Philip, the experienced one, explained how everything worked, but Richard was not happy, while Phil was noncommittal. Everything was set in Philip's way and the spinnaker filled perfectly until the wind practically died completely.

The argument as to what goes where will be continued on some future occasion I feel, particularly in rougher conditions. For the time being, however, we were reduced to motoring on a course well clear of St Albans Head. At about this time, mid-afternoon, Philip decided to try out our R.T. set by calling the coastguard at Portland.

As yet, of course, we had no call sign, nor had we had the installation tested. This would have to be done after our arrival home. I think that the rest of us felt slightly afraid of the set, or at any rate slightly embarrassed by the 'jargon' used. Philip sounded most professional as we all gazed open-mouthed while he informed the coastguard of our intentions.

Hearing "Coquette" called over the air for the first time was quite a thrill as we had been undecided about our final choice of name.

We now felt reassured and also sensed for the first time that this plastic container in which we dwelt was a boat with a definite character and we were beginning to trust her.

The uppermost thought in all our minds on this first day was to get past Portland Bill. As we proceeded on the engine due to a complete loss of wind, we got our first sight of Portland Bill, just a trifle hazy, but quite distinct in outline. We had set a course to pass five miles south of it.

We had no intention of telling horrific tales of being caught in the Portland Race.

When I say that we were on course, I should have mentioned 'Fred' our wonderful Nautec Autohelm. Fred really was superb even in really heavy seas and he certainly took the hard work out of helming. In all we motored for just over three hours, after which the wind piped up and we were surging along with the staysail and three reefs in the main – all or nothing, in fact.

We decided to split into watches for the night passage. Jack and Richard took over at 18:00 hrs, while Philip and Phil would come on at 21:00 hrs, at which time we would all endeavour to have our evening meal.

As there were five of us, I was excused doing a watch.

There was no doubt about it, I was the one and only cook. During our stay on the marina we had eaten well, even in some style, but I had warned of the likely deterioration in our standards.

I never spoke a truer word. The wind had increased to at least Force 6 and over, with the sea to match and work in the galley became difficult. We have a cooker with oven, but even with the little practice obtained during our brief trials, I found that in a Force 7 the oven door refused to remain closed. I mentioned this to the fitter who came to locate a gas leak while on the marina, but he didn't seem surprised or even concerned.

I was disappointed, as at first I had intended only having the usual grill and two burners.

However, I was strongly advised to have the full cooker by experienced cruising people. "You will have a pot full of stew across the cabin," they said, "much safer to cook it in the oven."

Using the oven, I had a chicken across the cabin and was jolly thankful that stew was not on the menu.

However, at some future time I may meet someone who can make the oven door keep closed.

So, on this occasion and all others on this trip, the pressure cooker was wonderful, well secured by the fiddle.

This first night, in desperation, I put everything I could find into the pressure cooker, i.e. a packet of soup and water, Surprise peas, a few stray mushrooms, a tin of corn and two tins of sliced lean beef. I eventually doled this out in soup bowls into which I had first put a mound of Smash dehydrated potatoes, and handed round spoons. It seemed the only way. It was received gratefully and duly devoured, but unknown to the others, my courage failed. It looked horrible. The 'sliced lean beef' was a greasy mass, although I did my best to remove the fat. While this concoction was cooking, I filled flasks with soup and made sandwiches to keep the night watches happy and awake.

I managed a sandwich for my supper, but I must admit that it was an effort and what was more I felt much happier up in the cockpit than down below, as did Philip. I stayed there until around 03:30 hrs, when I went below and dozed until 06:00hrs. I always find the sea at night fascinating as there seem to be so many more craft about than in the daytime. We had expected to see a lot of shipping in the channel, but to our surprise found that we had it almost to ourselves, or so it seemed. But at night it was different and identifying lights helped one to forget one's queasiness. One craft astern did give us some anxious moments and we kept taking bearings, but eventually he sheered off to starboard presumably going into Brixham. It was a clear night and all the expected lights, such as Start Point, appeared in the right places and we were able to get good fixes. Our 'Seafix' was excellent and gave us good radio bearings. Only the Log was stupid, the faster we went, the less it registered and vice versa.

Monday morning became bright and sunny. We were still running and going very well, but the seas were very big and there was a generally nasty motion. My breakfast speciality on these occasions is porridge. It is hot, not greasy, and very filling. The crew rapidly became addicts. I still felt a little queasy but I struggled to eat my, by this time, cold porridge which completely cured me for the rest of the trip. Philip soon gave up the struggle, and his porridge, twice over.

However, undaunted, he was still with it as regards the navigation.

The day followed much the same pattern as the previous one, and after a brisk start, we found that we had to motor again around midday.

I had the near-pleasure of washing up, having previously soaked the utensils in sea water.

Conservation of fresh water worried me rather as five people soon get through a few gallons.

Philip retired below and appeared to sleep, but returned when lunch was on the go. We lunched quite well on Anne's chicken. Philip's optimism was a trifle misplaced and he hastily retired to his bunk. A mystery now engrossed us, this being the whereabouts of the Eddystone Lighthouse. We couldn't even get a radio bearing of it, although we could get a signal from the Lizard, also a couple from the French coast.

We became convinced that we had been pushed too far south by wind and tide and we decided to alter course slightly more to the north.

We eventually found that we had originally been on our correct course, as when we did find land we had to alter course again slightly south. I suppose it is the old story – always trust your compass and don't believe what you see. Had the log been doing its thing we would never have accused *Coquette* of making so much leeway. Richard managed to get us a satisfactory fix and we headed happily towards Falmouth. He and Philip conferred as to whether we should proceed to Newlyn, but decided in favour of Falmouth.

Actually we settled for St Mawes, as it looked very easy to enter. We enquired of a passing yacht if there were any moorings available and were told that there were plenty.

We found a large mooring buoy with *Lady ?* painted on it and tied up to that. We couldn't have found a pleasanter spot to stay the night. The sun was shining, we had plenty of water under us, and the tree-lined shore and higgledy-piggledy village on the hillside were indeed a welcome sight. The dinghy was inflated and we made for the shore in the direction of a sailing club which was marked on the chart. We required water, diesel, bread and marmalade (a jar had spilled), We also wanted a nice hot shower or preferably a hot bath and to this end we went armed with towels and 'dolly bags'. The latter are what most people call toilet bags, but Jack has a dolly bag and I suspect the rest of the crew will have dolly bags for quite some time. The sailing club was not open and in any case it didn't look the sort of place where the visiting sailor could sit and soak up to his ears in hot water.

However, our first need was gratified as there was a cold water tap and the boys filled our cans.

Diesel was more difficult, but a friendly fisherman on finding that we only required about 11 gallons, said that Jack could go on board his boat which was anchored not far from us and help himself. On no account was he to touch the hooks. He didn't. £10 was handed over and everyone was happy.

Jack and Philip later collected their fuel from the boat and had a terrible job to find the tank at all due to the apparent chaos on board.

While these negotiations were going on, I hastened on ahead into St. Mawes on a bread hunt and as I approached the front I heard a great noise of chattering, like a flock of noisy starlings.

Sure enough a coach load of elderly ladies had staggered from their vehicle and were excitedly milling around the "Gifte Shoppes" of which there were plenty, but no bread shops. I couldn't help wondering why these ladies should bother to come to such an idyllic spot if all that they wanted were trinkets which they could have bought more easily in their local Co-op. They certainly paid no attention to their surroundings. A little later on I did begin to wonder about the sanity of our own way of life – after all, we all had comfortable homes.

After much bother, I did manage to buy what I imagined to be the last two loaves in St. Mawes, also marmalade and fruit. I met up with the rest of the gang who were happily sucking ice creams.

Philip had a wonderful idea. Why not book at a hotel for dinner (a nice change for the cook) and when one is cruising a decent hotel will always let sailors use their bathrooms? There were some attractive hotels, but they said that bathrooms were attached to bedrooms and all bedrooms were occupied.

Slightly dispirited we booked a table at a restaurant and subsequently had a very nice meal pleasantly served. The boys couldn't quite make up their minds whether to spend their funds on a good meal and have a moderate amount to drink, or whether to have fish and chips and a large quantity of booze. A compromise was reached. They would do their drinking while we returned to the boat to change and bring their 'good clothes' and we would eat together.

We sat on a wall discussing these arrangements and we all agreed that the wall was going up and down.

While the boys went to do the town, the rest of us repaired to the public conveniences, determined to clean ourselves up a bit. It was an impressive building, but I found neither hot water, soap, towels nor paper, also when the taps were turned the most extraordinary noises came from the plumbing.

Jack and Philip also had noises in their compartment, but found they could, by a combined effort, produce an interesting oom-pah-pah effect. I didn't ask who oomed and who pah'ed. Thus with difficulty and in my case the incredulity of a stray elderly lady, we made ourselves presentable.

We later phoned our families and after dinner returned early to the boat to catch up on sleep and prepare ourselves for an early start in the morning.

Jack was the first to roll into his bunk.

Philip was the last.

It seemed to fall to his lot to put our books away and remove our spectacles from our faces after we had fallen asleep.

In the middle of the night Jack got up to silence noises that no-one else had heard, in fact the radar deflector was banging against the shroud.

He fell off the step, dropped a washboard, kicked a bucket on deck, also sundry blocks and than returned in much the same manner.

In the morning he had the effrontery to complain that Philip was snoring!

We woke up just five minutes too late for the shipping forecast, but it was a beautiful morning with clear blue skies and at 0:740hrs we left the *Lady?* mooring under sail.

We were all well aware of the importance of catching the tide round Lands End. We required to go round at about 16:30hrs, so that we had plenty of time to get this right. We were soon abreast of St Anthony's Head and with relief passed the Manacles about which we had heard frightening stories. At about 10:30hrs. Philip contacted the Lizard coastguard who gave us a forecast of 5 - 6 N.E. veering E. We belted along still with only our staysail, not yet having seen our Nos 1 and 2 genoas. The boys were kept busy reefing and unreefing the main. After breakfast Phil found himself a bit short of sleep and retired below to put this right. Richard and Philip continued to get good fixes from the Lizard and around 15:00hrs we sighted the Wolf Rock Lighthouse on the port bow.

Everything was fine and we knew exactly where we were.

Philip called Land's End Radio and gave them particulars of our intentions. They asked for E.T.A. Anglesey but accepted Philip's explanation that as yet we were undecided whether to go to Milford Haven, the Irish coast or straight up to Holyhead. All depended on later conditions.

Land's End came into sight, also a dolphin and a coaster in the distance, who later came and gave us a friendly wave.

Phil came up just in time to see us turn right at Land's End.

We were disappointed with our view of the lighthouse. Such a symbolic mark should surely have been a nice bright white.

Jack especially, who I always feel was born with a paintbrush in his mouth, was disillusioned.

Anyway, shortly afterwards things began to happen; the wind really began to blow and the seas were quite something. The main was further reefed and for a time we were reduced to the storm sail, although with this we did find that we wallowed rather, and as soon as possible the staysail was substituted.

We elders were very grateful to our muscular juniors.

With Land's End left behind we roared into the night.

Preparing the evening meal was obviously going to be difficult, so I started operations early, sitting on the floor of the galley in order to stay in one spot. The cooker came and clouted me between the shoulder blades and the pressure cooker, half full of water, fell on my leg. I'll not forget to anchor it down again, my bruises will remind me.

All the cupboard doors in the cabin had by now flown open and deposited their contents around the cabin and we had secured their pretty brass knobs temporarily with elastic bands. There are adjustment screws, which obviously we will adjust when possible, but I did rather yearn for the sliding doors of our previous boat. I also rather coveted a safety strap for the galley so that I might remain upright to do my chores. Another hazard that I just avoided was an electric switch with a long pointed lever, which had been placed in the galley. I escaped with merely a slight bruise on my forehead, but could easily have injured my eye. I wonder who designs fittings for boats – presumably not people who sail.

During this most uncomfortable night we made various discoveries, the most serious being that the forward compartment was nearly awash. The boys had to bucket water out every hour. Their sleeping bags were soaked and general chaos reigned.

Jack eventually discovered the cause of this when we made

harbour. It was a small hole in the forepeak area, which he managed to successfully stop up with Araldite.

Another nasty hazard that threatened us was oily water seeping into the galley and main cabin from the engine well. To eliminate the obvious danger of slipperiness I had to scrub and scrub with washing up liquid and Brillo pads. All our shoes were affected and it took some time to de-oil them. We also had all-penetrating diesel in the cockpit. This had been caused by a slight overfilling of the tank. The surplus drained into the cockpit locker and in turn out of a drain hole in that to the cockpit.

Something will obviously be done about these minor irritations when we get the time. Another rather crafty little practical joker had put the overflow pipe from the water tank inside a cupboard in the cabin. After our first discovery of wet salt and sugar etc. we have become more cunning. Someone holds a cloth round the pipe and yells to the person pouring water on deck when it overflows. The particular problem is that Jack is slightly deaf, but we are improving our technique.

At about this stage of our trip I became aware of the boat's noises. I suppose every boat has its own individual sounds and one learns to accept them. Dozing in the starboard bunk and knowing from the conversations in the cockpit that we were a little short of radio bearings, I heard the distant clanging of a bell. The noise increased and then having reached a crescendo, gradually diminished. Simultaneously Richard dashed from the cockpit to the chart-table and back again. My curiosity got me up as I knew where we were and where we should not have been,

When I enquired about the bell, Richard and Jack looked at me pityingly and suggested I'd better lie down again. Towards the end of the trip, Phil also heard the bells – much to my relief. It was decided that the phenomenon was caused by the transducer.

Another strange noise that puzzled me, when in a semi-asleep state, was the distant sound of a choir, complete with tenor soloist.

The work being sung was not familiar, but though "modern"

was not unpleasant to my ears.

I kept quiet about this one until I'd solved the riddle. 'Fred' was, I think, the soloist and the choir came from the ventilators in the toilet area. The general effect was quite soothing.

This particular night after leaving Land's End was particularly wretched as the sea was really nasty and we had a Force 6 to contend with, at least.

I managed to make the usual "mess of potage" in the pressure cooker which was all eaten up.

The soup, which I made for the night watches, was a fiasco and was rejected by all. When I emptied the flasks next day, they were coated with thick grease.

These were the instant soups that I had used and which I have now thrown away. Philip had a rotten night and really looked rather grey. When, later, I asked him how he could enjoy sailing when he was ill in rough weather, his face lit up as he said, "It's wonderful!"

During the night there was some excitement as all our lights suddenly dimmed, including the navigation lights. The second battery (normally reserved for starting the engine) was switched on and our lights shone bright.

The engine was started in order to re-charge No 1 battery. At a later stage in the night about fifteen vessels were seen to be bearing down on us. However, a flash from the deck light and they all altered course by about 30 degrees.

Jack had made a very useful gadget for use on these occasions, in the form of a car spotlight with a handle attached which can be plugged in the cockpit. It is also useful when searching for moorings in the dark.

The next morning was not inspiring – a real grey dawn broke and the sky remained grey all day. We were naturally curious to know our position. Without a log this was a bit tricky, but Richard eventually got an R.D. bearing from Tusker Rock and, I think, Kinsale, which suggested that we were about 50 miles south of Tusker.

The shipping forecast was for 4 - 5 N.E. and rain likely.

We plodded on during a cold day through very big seas. We saw lots of gannets, also Manx Shearwaters and Storm Petrels. The gannets were really spectacular and were often in groups of ten or more.

To-day's interesting episode was the discovery that the main bilge was pretty full and that the pump would not empty it. Eleven buckets were baled out plus sundry bits of wood and other material. When we reached harbour Jack found that the pump was clogged with debris and, after cleaning, it was prepared to function.

Weather conditions worsened – should we reduce to the storm jib again?

Philip remained alone in the cockpit in the rain. He felt better up there, which was lucky for the rest of us, as at least it was warm and dry below. We have a photo of him doing his solo act. He wondered if the time had come when we should have to hoist the storm jib, but the general decision was that it was better to keep going as long as possible.

Eventually Richard decided that the time had indeed come and we luffed up in order to effect the change. Our Leistay and halyards leading to the cockpit do minimise the difficulties at these times.

The wind was now a quite definite Force 7 and going up to 8. The waves were to match.

We still fairly roared along – no wallowing this time – just slicing through the waves.

A lively lady is *Coquette*, and we had by now really learnt to trust her. Richard, the acknowledged expert with the R.D.F., said that we were almost directly on course for Dunmore East.

Very soon we sighted Ireland, which came towards us all too rapidly in the form of two islands and sundry rocks. We also had seen what we thought was a trawler, but in such big waves it was difficult to be sure. Unfortunately, our chart of the area was only a small-scale one and it made close recognition difficult. We prudently stood off to sea again while our navigators struggled manfully.

Jack saw a couple of fishing boats, which he felt sure were going home and that we should follow them. But we didn't know where their home was.

Philip, who had been preserving his status quo by staying in the cockpit, now showed true gallantry. He came below and tried to call the trawlers on our starboard bow. There was no reply. Then suddenly a voice was calling "Coquette" in the form of the Dunmore Pilot.

His was indeed a sweet voice. Philip, still preserving his, and indeed all our dignity, refrained from saying that we were lost, instead asked to have our position confirmed, mentioning the two islands and saying that our log was not working.

The islands were, as we had imagined, the Saltees. It appeared that the trawler we had seen earlier was no other than the Konigsberg Lightship. It would have been easier in the dark, really.

Dumore Pilot didn't seem enthusiastic about our going to Dunmore East, but suggested that we later contact Rosslare Harbour. Philip politely thanked him and was equally politely sick over the side. Four grown men now decided to carry on non-stop to Anglesey. The cook let it be known that to go back into "that" all night, when we could more easily spend a night in a comfortable harbour, seemed madness to her.

After all, two of these grown men were not young and one of them was not having too happy a time.

The cook retired to her bunk and became fatalistic.

Some sort of conference was going on aloft and then the motion of the boat became pleasanter. They had decided to put into Dunmore East to give me a night's rest, and I suppose that I was as good an excuse as any.

Without too much difficulty we got into Dunmore East and aided by our spotlight found a berth alongside another boat. The owners very kindly helped us to tie up and were thrilled to know that we had come from Lymington. They themselves were from Poole, but were leaving at 06:00hrs the next day for Cork.

We had a good supper - it was so easy.

Phil, whose birthday it was, was anxious to go ashore and sample Guinness. Our neighbours said that we needn't worry about the pubs closing as we were in Ireland, but the difficulty would be in getting ashore. Short of blowing up the dinghy, there was no way. Phil almost tried a standing 12-foot leap up the harbour wall, but even he admitted defeat in the end.

Philip insisted on washing up, which made me feel rather guilty, but I really appreciated it.

The next morning the forecast was for N.E. 4-5, veering S.E.

We all went on deck and helped to untie ourselves from our neighbours. On their other side was a 40ft Catamaran from Victoria B.C. with a man and woman and two small children on board. They had been in Europe for three years and were going to sail back home.

We rather sadly left Dunmore East with its colony of Kittiwakes, having first filled up with water. I think that we would all have liked to spend some time cruising around Southern Ireland.

It wasn't too bad a morning and we were very soon abreast of the Konigsberg Lightship, which was duly photographed, and we set a course for Tusker Rock. Philip had I think really found his sea legs by now and was ready for anything. In fact he was ready to try and calculate our speed, having noticed that Jack had a pocket calculator on board. The first idea was a calculation using a dropped match over the bow and timed at the stern, but the intervening 32 ft didn't seem enough for real accuracy. The young brains thought an object tied on a known length of line and trailed astern until taut was better. A piece of line was measured, but a suitable object seemed difficult to find. A beer can seemed right, so the boys set about emptying one. A reading was obtained by this method, but unfortunately the beer can was lost on the haul in. It was a little early in the morning for too much beer can emptying, so I offered them my second best wooden spoon.

This proved to be the best object so far, and several readings were taken and results calculated.

Two facts emerged – first that our watches were not completely reliable, and second that the log was crackers.

We sighted Tusker Rock then set our course for Wales and the last leg of our journey.

The day passed uneventfully and calmly and we had a reasonable lunch and dinner, even having a sweet at the latter.

We got organised for the night. We were on this leg tacking as we had an easterly wind, so progress was fairly slow.

As usual the wind increased during the night and during Phil's watch he put six reefs in the main.

Jack and Richard's watch proved to be really rough and no one got any sleep, I think. There was a rather anxious period when a ship appeared to be on a collision course. They flashed lights, but to no avail and our speed was really fantastic. The offending vessel passed in front rather closer than one would have chosen. There seemed no question of a power vessel giving way to sail.

Quite suddenly at around 04:00hrs the wind died and the sea settled.

The wind was so slight now, and on the nose, that we sadly decided to motor in order to catch the tide from Holyhead to Puffin. Philip was at last able to contact Anglesey Radio and reported our position. When we eventually got a reliable fix we were rather disappointed to find that we were about eight miles further from Holy Island than we had thought.

However, we were now on the home stretch so we pressed on as fast as possible and did manage to catch the tide off Holyhead.

We had an hour or two in the early morning when the motion was really appalling in a large sea and it was some time before I could even manage to produce porridge, which was a shame as it was the first time that Philip was really enthusiastic about his breakfast. Still, I'm sure that he was pleased with his triumph of mind over matter.

The race off Carmel Head was quite lively and Richard, after expressing his thanks to 'Fred' for all his good work, took over from him.

Once more we checked the log by the familiar mile off Bull Bay.

I think we were expecting some miracle from our own measured mile, perhaps thinking that the southern ones were in some way different.

However, the results were the same. After passing the oil terminal off Amlwch we at last hoisted sails and had a very pleasant reach up to Puffin, where as so often, the wind died. So we finally packed up the sails and started collecting our gear. Strangely enough two items were missing – Philip's shoes, which so often had either singly or united, clattered around the galley, and our hold-all. Happily, later in the week I found these articles, which were in their right places.

On reaching Beaumaris we found that our mooring was occupied, also Tony's, so we picked *Bona Deals* mooring up for the time being. Apparently no-one had expected us due to the rotten forecasts down south.

We unloaded our gear on to the pier and were delighted to find Anne waiting for us there. She had had faith, also a feeling that we would come on that tide. We all struggled up to the cottage and started a bath rota, then had a free and easy meal sitting on chairs and the floor around the lounge while we struggled to keep awake for our reminiscences.

It had been a satisfying experience, mainly because the boat had been really well tried out and we were all delighted with her. Our two wonderful aids were the Seafix R.D.F. (without which where would we have been?) and the Nautec Autohelm, 'Fred'. He really tackled anything that was thrown at him, and he had plenty.

For ourselves, well we've all learnt a good deal and are looking forward to so many things. It was a wonderful trip this first one, and worth remembering.

Sheila Orrell

CHAPTER 9

CRUISE TO IRELAND

HAVING *COQUETTE*, our new Contessa 32, safely home, Sheila and I decided that we were now sufficiently experienced to risk a solo cruise to Dunlaoghaire.

Our good friends Tony and Margaret Stromberg asked if they could accompany us in their yacht *Arian Mor*, a 30ft Anderson design that Tony had built himself. We were very happy to have their company.

There was only a very gentle breeze when we set off, so we had to motor for the first two hours, after which a moderate Force 3-4 helped us on our way.

We arrived in Dunlaoghaire at about 16:00hrs and anchored outside the yacht club. We inflated our dinghy, clipped on our Mariner outboard and motored ashore. After a wander around the sights, we joined our friends in the club for a few drinks, and then had dinner.

Tony had anchored close to us, and we were awakened early next morning by howls of rage. His dinghy had sprung a leak and deflated during the night, and had drowned his Seagull outboard. Tony was a mechanical wizard and within the hour had stripped it down, dried it out and got it running once again – something you can do with a Seagull as they are very basic and simple engines. You'll never believe it – he drowned it again the next day

Tony and Margaret decided that they would stay on for a few days, but I had to get back for work next week so we had to return on our own. By the time we had reached Holyhead, we were glad we had started really early, as the wind had increased to Force 5 and the sea was covered in great 'white horses'. It was now

20:00hrs and in these conditions I decided that we had better put in to the harbour for the night. The sea wasn't much calmer in the harbour, as we motored around looking for a mooring to pick up. The difficulty was that the strong wind and tide was making all the boats lie close to each other.

One of us had got to run forward with the boat hook and catch the marker buoy, pull it in, and make the line fast on the bow cleat. It was a question of which one. I didn't want Sheila to have to do it, as in these conditions, unless you are strong and really quick to make it fast, you can either lose it or lose a couple of your fingers.

With trepidation she volunteered to take the helm. I ran forward with the boat hook, but unfortunately she overran the buoy twice and nearly clouted the next boat.

On the third run through the moorings I managed to catch the buoy, and above the wind screamed to her to cut the engine. I just managed to get a turn on the cleat and made fast... Phew – it was not funny!

We retired below for a double Scotch.

When we looked out in the early morning the wind had abated to a Force 3, so we wasted no time in washing up and having breakfast but cast off the mooring, hoisted our sails and completed our leg back to Beaumaris.

We were well pleased with our weekend cruise and the pointing ability of our new boat.

CHAPTER 10

VIEW OF THE SEA

BY THIS TIME you will probably realise that we are not normal stable people.

We had been happy at the Old Barracks Cottage for a few years. We had a delightful walled garden and a charming house, but we had no view. We had been spoiled in West Kirby by having a superb position on the sea front and we began to miss it. We started to scan the local papers each week in the hope of finding a suitable house which would satisfy our craving.

One gorgeous summer's evening we decided to go for a walk from Beaumaris along the beach in the direction of Puffin Island. At that time there was a full-size offshore lifeboat stationed in Beaumaris. It was housed in a shed about half a mile from the town on the way to Puffin Sound. Close to it and right on the shore there was a house owned by a Mr Girling, who at one time had been a member of the lifeboat crew. He was now in his seventies, and was sitting on the launching slipway, puffing away at his pipe and enjoying the glorious sunset for which the Menai Straits is famous.

"Evening, Mr Girling," I said. "What a lovely day it's been! You're lucky living in a super spot like this; if you ever think of selling, please give me the first option."

"No, I'm not thinking of selling, but there's an empty cottage a little way along the beach, and I do believe that it's for sale," he replied.

We couldn't get along the beach quick enough. The property in question appeared to be an old fisherman's cottage which had at some time had an upstairs extension added to it. It was in a bad state of repair and from the 50 milk bottles outside we judged that

53

it had probably been let out as a holiday home.

Nothing daunted, I rang the owner and arranged to collect the key and carry out an inspection. When we looked round we decided that it would have to be completely gutted, with all new windows, doors, roof and heating, for a start. It was obviously going to cost thousands and thousands – and years of hard work – to put it right, but the situation, right on virtually a private beach, was the best in all Anglesey. Outside, the grounds were three feet high in weeds and there was not a flower in sight.

There was no comparison, of course, with the beautiful Old Barracks Cottage which had been completely rebuilt, and the asking price was approximately what we estimated that The Barracks was worth.

As you will know by now, I am an impetuous individual and quickly made up my mind. We were absolutely enchanted. We didn't argue about the price and signed the contract the next day. We didn't bother about a survey, as we knew it would be a waste of money.

We advertised The Barracks in the *Liverpool Daily Post*, and sold it within a fortnight to Peter Dickey, the managing director of the famous Boat Building Company.

When we moved in to Minnows we were thrilled with the magnificent view from every window in the house; however they were multi-paned wooden windows and we soon realised that they had reached their sell-by date, were riddled with wood rot, and would have to be replaced.

We contacted Eddie Davies of Anglesey Glass and arranged to have the whole house fitted with aluminium double-glazed windows.

The next thing was tackling the damp problem. For this we had a specialist firm knock out all the plaster and install an Electros system, which consisted of a series of titanium wires connected in an electric loop system throughout the stonework

The house had been heated by a number of night storage heaters, which we found were providing hardly any heat by the evening, so we installed an oil-fired heating system with 17 radiators.

All this took time, and whilst it was being done I set to work to sort out the garden and outbuildings. I managed to secure the services of Ken Thomas, the master builder who had re-built the Old Barracks Cottage.

We decided that a fire-damaged chalet in the grounds, which was in an equally dilapidated condition, would need a completely new ship-lapped wooden front, so he and I set to work. We ripped out the burnt wood and fitted all new wood, then replaced the door and windows.

Ken worked for me for years on and off, and constructed a double garage, Welsh slate patios, and amongst other things, a new block consisting of a large bedroom on the ground floor, complete with its adjoining bathroom suite. I enjoy practical work, so I put in a pine ceiling, and did a complete tiling job.

The garden, as I stated before, was non-existent. One of the previous owners had laid a large gravel driveway, which was fine in itself but the contractors must have ordered twice as much foundation stone as was necessary, and so had dumped all the surplus over what had once been a lawn.

I bought a heavy duty Clifford Rotary Cultivator, and spent most of the winter going over the area completely, and then removing the stones which it churned up. I then borrowed a tractor and chain harrows from my neighbour, levelled out the ground, and then sowed it with lawn seed. Unfortunately more weeds than grass was the result, and it took years to produce any semblance of a lawn.

CHAPTER 11

MAJORCA

WHEN THEY RETIRED, Ken and Audrey Livingstone, two of our great sailing friends, decided to sail their yacht *Bouzouki* over to Majorca. They liked it so much that they bought a flat in St Telmo, a lovely little resort on the south coast of the island.

Sheila and I decided to take a holiday, go over and see how they were getting on.

They gave us a great welcome when we arrived. They had moored their yacht at Puerto Andraitx, so they used to pick us up from our hotel and take us out sailing to all the beautiful bays around the island, where we would anchor, dive overboard into the warm crystal clear water and then enjoy our lunch, which was usually washed down with a bottle of Rioja at about £2 a bottle.

Thursday was market day at Andraitx, so we used to meet up with a crowd of their friends outside one of the cafés in the square, and enjoy a delicious Majorcian lunch whilst trying to make conversation in a mixture of English, French and Spanish.

Bernard and Rowena Halle, some more of our sailing friends, had also sailed their yacht there and decided to settle down. They had purchased a small estate, which consisted of an orchard of old olive trees and a ruined farmhouse, which they were in the course of rebuilding.

Majorca is a beautiful island and Palma, the capital with its magnificent cathedral, myriads of crooked little streets and palatial squares, really won our hearts.

Close to where Ken and Audrey had their flat, a block of 12 apartments was being built, so I said to Sheila, "Let's go and have a look."

Oh no! Here we go again…

The building was three storeys high and was nearing completion. The apartments had two bedrooms, a fully tiled bathroom, a 22ft lounge which opened on to a large balcony and a luxury bathroom. They also had a basement store room and a garage. On the ground floor there was a large open air swimming pool. The balcony had a lovely view across the bay to Dragonera Island.

It transpired that all the apartments had already been sold, with the exception of one which was on the middle floor. The asking price seemed very reasonable; and we were by now having visions of lounging in deck chairs on that balcony. The next day we went to see the selling agents in Puerto Andraitx. The office manager was a very smart German lady called Margot, who promptly offered us a £500 reduction in the asking price if we made a deposit by the end of the week.

We discussed it all day and eventually decided that perhaps we could afford it and that it would be nice to be able to offer it to our children and their families for holidays – so we bought it.

That was the easy bit. We had been told that our apartment would be ready for occupation in about two months. I kept ringing up from England and was subjected to months of excuses for the delay.

Eventually Margot informed us that only a few finishing touches remained; so we decided that the time had come to go over and investigate

Fitting out a new house or apartment is always a busy time and evolves lots of journeying backwards and forwards to pick up all the little necessities, so instead of flying out there we decided to go by car.

At this time I was running a Triumph Stag, which was an open two-seater with a very small seat at the back. It wasn't yet two years old and was a delightful car to drive; the only snag was that it was unreliable and the engine used to over-heat – not ideal for travelling to a hot climate. Reluctantly, I did a swap for a new Opel Rekord hatchback. It wasn't as glamorous but was more sensible

Our new Opel Rekord hatchback.

for conveying loads of gear to foreign parts.

Having loaded our new acquisition with pots and pans, blankets and all the other necessities we could think of, we sallied forth bound for Dover.

I was now retired, so time was not a factor and we were looking forward to the drive across France. We had not booked any accommodation, and when we landed at Calais decided to spend the night at Neufchatel. It was only a small village with one hotel, which offered us a bed for the night. The bedroom was quite small but had an enormous suite in dark mahogany and a bed with a headboard which reached almost up to the ceiling.

When we asked about dinner, we were told that the chef had gone home for the night; but if we were lucky we might get a meal at the café down the road. We dashed down there only to find that they were closing for the night; but unlike our own country folk, they said they would do what they could for us and would an omelette be all right ?

By this time we were very hungry so we accepted their kind offer. The omelette turned out to be a super affair, surrounded by mushrooms, and a salad; this was followed by huge pieces of apple pie, ice cream, coffee, and a bottle of wine. Not bad, as they were supposed to be closed!

The next day we were up bright and early to continue our journey across France.

We were delighted to find how uncongested the ordinary roads were, compared with the British Isles, and marvelled at the numerous places of rest, which included decent toilet facilities. The next night found us in Argenton-sur-Creuse, another village with only two small hotels to choose from. The first one drew a blank, so it was with trepidation that I rang the little bell on the reception desk of the other one. Yes! They would be able to accommodate us for the night; we could have a meal in the bar but would have to sleep in a building down the road.

We were very intrigued when we got there, to find that it looked like a warehouse and there didn't appear to be anybody else in residence. The bedroom we had been allotted was enormous, and contained three double beds. There was a screen in the middle of the room and at the back of the screen there was an old fashioned tin bath. Tired as we were we didn't feel like making use of this facility.

The toilet was down a narrow corridor, and was illuminated by a delayed action system, so if you occupied it for more than two minutes you had to grope your way back to the bedroom in complete darkness. Sheila was not amused but we had no alternative, so we just "grinned and beared it".

Having tidied ourselves up, we went along to the pub wondering what sort of a meal we would get. We needn't have worried – the landlord and the inmates couldn't have been nicer and started us off with large bowls of delicious French onion soup, followed by steak and chips, pancakes and coffee,

When we had finished our meal we found that there was a real party atmosphere developing, and the wine was flowing like water. A piano, a fiddle and an accordion appeared from nowhere, and we were the guests of honour.

After two of our new friends had sung for us, in French of course, I was asked to give an English contribution to the party.

Way back in earlier days Sheila had decided that I had quite a good voice; and as she was an accomplished pianist, we used to practice duets together. Anyway I gave them a rendering of "Sea Fever", and it appeared to go down pretty well as they wouldn't let me off without an encore – so I sang them "Shenandoah". It was a spontaneous and lovely evening, and we finally stumbled down to our funny bedroom at about 2:00am. Two of the party were apparently off-duty Gendarmes, and presented me with a special hat with the French Cockerel on it.

It was a bleary-eyed couple who came down to breakfast the next morning.

My old army boozing nights must have given me an immunity which obviously impressed the landlord, as he offered me a glass of brandy with my breakfast. The staff came out and waved us a cheery goodbye and we were off on another long day's journey.

We had a very good clear run, only stopping for a sandwich lunch, and by evening arrived near to Toulouse.

We came across a charming little hotel on the way, so decided to stop there rather than go into the town, where parking for strangers might be more difficult.

We were fortunate this time and had a super four-course 'gourmet' dinner which we shared with an interesting German couple, who were intending to do a walk around Brittany.

Apparently it was some sort of national holiday the next day, as the hotel was going to be closed and there would be no staff. We were told that our breakfast would be on the table and that when we left would we please see that the hotel was locked up

We did seem to end up in queer places!

For our next leg, we wanted to reach the coast so that we would have an easy approach to dockland at Barcelona, where we would be joining our ship for the crossing to Palma.

We had a lovely day's run through the beautiful wine-growing country close to Carcassone and stopped in the magnificent old walled city to inspect the fortifications and also have a meal. In the early evening we arrived at Perpignan, which we had calculated would be the ideal place to spend the night, so that in the morning we would have an easy run in to Barcelona.

Perpignan was a pleasant little seaside resort and we managed to book in to a hotel on the promenade. We even had a bedroom with a sea view.

At last we arrived at Barcelona. We were a little worried about finding our way to the docks, but it was well sign-posted, and more or less a straight run in.

Once our car was safely parked on board, we did a tour of the nicely appointed, spacious ship, and ended up in the dining saloon for a well-deserved late lunch.

Disembarking was no problem, as the dock at Palma leads straight on to the promenade.

The drive to St Telmo takes about an hour, and of course one had to get used to driving on the right-hand side of the road once again.

It was great to be back in the glorious sunshine and we were really excited as we drove up the hill to our apartment.

We had a lovely big garage underneath the apartment, so I drove down there and with trepidation inserted the key we had been sent into the lock. Hey presto, it fitted and the three-inch thick pine door disappeared into the roof. We emptied all our luggage onto the garage floor and then started to take some of the cases up to our second floor apartment.

Margot had kindly arranged to have an electric cooker and an enormous fridge installed; she had also bought us a double bed and mattress for one of the bedrooms so at least we would have somewhere to sleep for the first night,

We had no idea what sort of condition the builders would have left things in, as of course it was brand new.

As in most Spanish apartments all the floors were tiled, and the first thing I noticed was that they were covered in cement... We were obviously going to have a busy time, as all the workmen had now left the site.

We were very tired after our long drive and sorting things out, so we didn't do very much the first day, except to make a note of all visible faults and what was necessary to correct them.

The next day we were up bright and early, and drove into Palma to purchase all the bits and pieces which are necessary to furnish a new home. It would have to be done in easy stages.

Palma is a fascinating city, with a labyrinth of narrow streets and alleyways. We had a whale of a time, examining dozens of oriental rugs, exotic lamps and other items.

We ended up ordering a large bamboo table with matching chairs, a bamboo lounge suite, a cane cocktail cabinet, a set of small tables and two single beds for the other bedroom. These larger items would have to be delivered; but we stacked up the car with all sorts of electric gadgets, bathroom cupboards and so on, and we left Palma for our journey back to St Telmo with the roof festooned with two large rugs and a standard lamp.

The next few days were spent sand-papering the cement off the floors, giving all the pine woodwork another coat of varnish, and generally sorting things out.

Plumbing is not a strong point in Spain, and after we had got the cement out of the bath, we found that the WC wouldn't function. We managed to locate a plumber, and he seemed to be well aware of the problem, as he inserted some sort of "bomb" in it which went off with a terrific bang and apparently blew through the drains. We wondered what would happen to any of our neighbours if they happened to be using the facilities at the same time! It was a bit drastic but it worked.

Once we had got things really straight, we invited Ken and Audrey and a number of our new friends in for a housewarming. Gin at that time was about £2 a bottle, so as you can imagine everyone ended up very happy.

The apartments faced south, and each had its own open balcony with a lovely view across to Dragonera Island. We proceeded to fill ours with bougainvillea and other exotic plants, and it was

SOME OF MY BOATS

Left:
Our second
Liverpool Bay
Falcon –
"Levant"

Right:
Sunset on
the straits
("Magic
Dragon")

Left:
Hustler 35
– "Fiddler of
Orwell"

Left: Bayliner 22 – cabin cruiser

Right: Frigate 27 – "Gun Smoke"

Left: "Magic Dragon" – Moody 33

Right: "Magic" – Westerly Pageant.

Below: "Titch" – Mirror dinghy.

*Below: "Coquette"
– Contessa 32*

Right:
"Fiddler of Orwell"

Left:
Catch 22 – Gambit

Right:
Finsailer 37
– Jansfin

Above and below: Our garden at Minnows, showing the summer-house and one of the ponds.

Sheila and I at my 90th birthday celebrations, June 2005.

Another view of the garden at Minnows.

Above: another picture of my 90th birthday party.
Below: Our daughter-in-law Anne, daughter Jane, son Robert and daughter Anne retire to the kitchen during the party.

The guests drink a toast...

With Sheila in the garden, March 2004.

amazing how quickly they started to grow.

Down below there was a large communal swimming pool and shower. Nearly all the other owners were Majorcians who lived and worked in Palma and only came down at the weekend, so we had the pool to ourselves for most of the week..

At about 9pm on Fridays, a stream of cars used to arrive and the week-end *fiesta* would begin. Spanish people only come to life after midnight and we didn't always feel like partying until 3am, so very often we had to resort to ear plugs to get any sleep.

They really were delightful friendly people, and would overwhelm us with gifts of fruit, wine, and gorgeous flowers.

The area surrounding the apartments had not been landscaped, so they used to bring with them an array of gardening tools and hundreds of plants. On Saturday mornings we all used to muck in and dig, cultivate and plant. However, it wasn't all slog: bottles of wine appeared from nowhere to invigorate us and a happy, carefree atmosphere prevailed.

St Telmo has a lovely little sandy beach and most days we would join our friends, alternately sunbathing and going for a swim.

As we had brought our car over we were able to make use of their local knowledge and explore the island from to bottom. Ken and Audrey's tiny Fiat had its doors tied on with string, and was ready for the scrap heap, so they were always happy to join us.

Bernard and Rowena Halle who, as I said, had retired to the island, had bought a semi-ruin in Formentor, engaged a local stone mason and were busily restoring it to its former glory. They had quite a bit of land with it and dozens of old olive trees, so we used to go and help them pick the fruit, and generally move bits of old masonry around. The restoration took quite a while to finish but when completed it was quite unique, with a magnificent modern kitchen full of concealed lights, and a lounge with a super stone fireplace going right up into the ceiling.

On a visit two years later we had the great pleasure of having one of Rowena's gourmet dinners in the completed masterpiece. They were real animal lovers and had brought their two Alsatians over from England. Not only that but Rowena had a habit of collecting strays every time they went to Palma, so in all I think they had five dogs and three cats.

CHAPTER 12

'MAGIC DRAGON'

COQUETTE WAS a lovely classical boat and with her long slim lines received admiring glances wherever we took her. She was fast and very stable, and we really enjoyed racing her. There was one snag, however. We were now doing more cruising than racing, and very often were taking friends with us. The accommodation on *Coquette* for more than three people was somewhat inadequate. She had six berths but on a long cruise they were claustrophobic. The 'heads' (toilet) was only enclosed by a plastic curtain and this could be embarrassing.

We decided to have a Moody 33 built.

The Moody though only a foot longer was beamier and considerably more comfortable. She had centre cockpit wheel steering and a rear twin cabin. In addition to four forward berths she also had a fully enclosed heads and a heated shower. We had to wait nine months for delivery.

She was launched near Northwich on the Manchester Ship Canal and our great friend Peter Ralli, who was a Ship Canal pilot, joined us on the occasion, and later guided us out into the River Mersey at Eastham. In view of our Welsh home, we named her *Magic Dragon*.

It had been quite a nice sunny and warm day in the sheltered canal, but when we finally reached the mouth of the Mersey at midnight, it was pitch black, and blowing Force 6,

We had to reef right down, and had quite an exciting delivery trip back to our mooring at Beaumaris.

Once we had sorted out all the new gear and provisioned her, we invited our old friend Dr Philip Robinson, who was a consultant

73

"Magic Dragon" on the River Weaver at Northwich.

at Clatterbridge Hospital, and another old friend Sam Davidson, an E.N.T. Specialist, to join us in a cruise up to Scotland .

Our first stop was at Port St Mary on the Isle of Man. It turned out to be quite a calm sea, with about a Force 3, so it was quite a gentle 'shake-down'.

Before we reached the harbour we dropped our sails, and motored in. It's always best to have a good look around to find a convenient spot near to a wall ladder.

The harbour was largely occupied by a fleet of fishing boats, so we waited until we saw three sailing boats rafted up together, and hailed them for permission to moor alongside.

It's necessary first of all to take fore and aft lines, right up on to the harbour wall and then to put on 'springs', which as I said before are short fore and aft lines running between your boat and your neighbour's. Large fenders are then put out to separate the two boats. If the harbour is crowded this can involve clambering over six or seven boats and climbing up a seaweed covered vertical steel ladder which is attached to the harbour wall (not funny if you arrive in the dark, and it's pouring with rain).

We had a day of rest, and did a tour of the island before going for a meal at the Bay View Hotel; their fresh crab was delicious.

The next day, was up to Port Patrick. This is always a popular resting place as it is a very well-sheltered harbour and the home of the offshore lifeboat which serves the coast; there is also a super little pub right on the quayside. There is a small pottery, so if one stops there on the way home it's useful for buying last minute-presents. We were now well on the way and thoroughly enjoying ourselves . The 'boys' had taken possession of the stern cabin and were very happy there; so Sheila and I had the luxury of sleeping in the rest of the boat, and also having a willing crew to share the chores.

The next day as we headed for Ghia we had a brisk north westerly right on the nose, so part of the way we dropped the genoa, reefed down the main and motored.

There is no real harbour in Ghia. The wind had raised rows of 'white horses' so we dropped our largest CQR anchor, backed off, and made sure it had really dug in before we inflated our Avon dinghy, attached the outboard engine and motored ashore.

We had not been misinformed and Ghia really is a paradise island. It is only about two miles long, and there is only one shop, which besides being a post office, is an Aladdin's cave of useful everyday things, such as spades, pots and pans, fishing gear, all the usual food items and even rows of malt whiskies. It also rents out ancient bicycles.

At the southern end of the island there is a delightful sandy beach for bathing and a large seal colony. There is no industry apart from a creamery, where cheese is made.

The main attraction of the island is its large botanical garden which is ablaze with thousands of prize specimens, some of which it is possible to purchase.

We spent two days on Ghia, and it was with sorrow in our hearts that we had to say farewell.

On our last night we had a super binge and dinner at the lovely little island hotel.

Leaving Ghia behind us, we sailed up the Sound of Jura to the Isle of Luing and Ardenama Bay. This was a favourite anchorage for the Venturers and we had heard many tales about it.

It was a very sheltered and safe mooring, but the entrance to it was very precarious on anything other than high water. It consisted of a shallow passage between a marker buoy and a narrow reef of rocks, so it was necessary to set up your approach with great care.

The guardian of the bay was Irene, an elderly Scottish lady who spoke with a very broad accent, wore trousers and had a man's haircut. She lived in a large house within the bay and used to sit by the window with a pair of binoculars, somewhat akin to a spider, and on the arrival of a yacht at the entrance, would charge out, and in no mean terms denigrate any unfortunate skipper who was making the wrong approach.

Once one had gained entrance and was safely anchored, it used to be amusing to see her waving her arms about, and roaring out, "What a shower!"

Actually she was very kind-hearted when you got to know her and besides offering tea and biscuits, would impart lots of useful local knowledge.

Everyone was invited into her sparsely-furnished front parlour, and were not allowed to escape without signing her big red book which held a record of the names of all the skippers, and their boats, that had entered the bay. In the following years I think we had nine visits entered.

About two miles around the coast, there was a renowned café which had been recommended by Irene. It concentrated on only doing evening meals, and alternated from week to week with either venison or Scotch salmon as a main course.

We asked Irene if she would phone and book us in for a meal. Unfortunately it turned out to be a very wet evening, so the café kindly sent their decrepit Land Rover over to pick us up. About 10 people were trying to get aboard, so Sheila and Philip decided that there was a short cut across the fields and that they would rather walk.

When we got to the café there was no sign of the intrepid couple, in spite of their short cut and they eventually turned up about 30 minutes later looking somewhat distraught. Apparently the short cut was across a field which was occupied by an enormous bull and his harem and he had staked his claim by making a running charge in their direction.

Sheila with her farming background and knowledge of how dangerous bulls can be, had advised a wide detour – so that was the cause of their late arrival. The sight of large gin and tonics soon seemed to make them forget their adventure.

Many years later, when we had retired from sailing due to *anno domini*, we went up to Scotland by car and hired a cottage on Seil Island. In nostalgic mood, we took a picnic and all our painting gear, and made our way to Adenama Bay. The highland cattle were still there splashing around in the shallows and providing us with an ideal painting project, but we were saddened to find the garden of Irene's house waist-high in weeds, and all the windows boarded up.

When we got back to our cottage, we went along to the old pub by the Bridge Over The Atlantic, and made inquiries about Irene. Apparently social services had decided that she had become too old to be left in her isolated house and had re-housed her in a hostel in Oban. It seems that she had taken on a new lease on life, and was enjoying the warmth and comfort of town life.

Pouldoran, which indeed was on Seil Island, was our next anchorage; this again was a very sheltered spot, with a one-way entrance. The only trouble was getting our anchor to hold as the bottom was covered in great masses of kelp (an octopus-like weed). The surrounding bog was alive with hundreds of yellow Flag Irises and it really was a delightful place to be.

Once we were settled in we rowed ashore and beached our dinghy.

The local pub, which was near the bridge, was reached by a

rough path about half a mile over the sand dunes. It was easy in daylight but fraught with danger when returning to the boat in the pitch dark, having sampled a good selection of the 35 single malt whiskys which lined the bar. The air was blue with grunts and curses, as our merry crew stumbled back to the dinghy.

The next day was lovely and sunny, so as Oban was only a short distance away we decided to spend it there, and do a spot of re-provisioning. When we arrived we found that there was a regatta in progress, so we were unlucky in finding a harbourside berth and had to pick up a mooring, which meant that we had to go ashore in our dinghy.

Oban is an important city, and has a fine harbour in which the McBrain ferries operate, running cruises to all the Isles.

Whilst we were there we had a surprise visit from Philip's son, David. Apparently he was crewing on one of the racing yachts. We were having afternoon tea in the cockpit when suddenly a large rubber dinghy roared up. It was David – he had been on board his yacht and had noticed our arrival in the harbour. We had the pleasure of his company for dinner that night.

Our main aim on this cruise was to reach Tobermory on the Isle of Mull. It was a favourite rendezvous of the Venturers and we had been advised of all the best haunts to visit whilst there. It would be a fairly long leg to put in a day, so we made a nice early start.

On the way we called in at Loch Aline and sailed for about an hour into the interior; towards the far end we encountered large areas of kelp which were getting entangled in our rudder so we turned around and continued our sail towards Tobermory.

There was a good constant Force 4-5 wind on the beam all the way so we had a cracking sail and arrived in Tobermory Harbour in the late afternoon.

We were not disappointed. All the hotels and shops on the waterfront were painted in pastel shades of pink, yellow, blue and orange, which created a real continental atmosphere.

Once again we were lucky, as apparently it was Regatta Week and the harbour was packed with magnificent racing yachts. This of course made it difficult to find a decent spot for anchoring, and we had no option but to accept a place which was some distance from the harbour wall; which meant that we had along run in the dinghy every time we wanted to go ashore.

Anchoring in a crowded harbour is quite a tricky business, as one has to visualise what effect the wind and tide will have on your position with regard to your neighbours, as you don't want to find that you are banging into another boat in the middle of the night. It's best to steer clear of all motor boats if you can, as they swing at a much faster rate than a sailing boat.

Having made sure that we were safely anchored, we headed for the 'flesh pots'. When we reached the harbour wall, we found that the iron railings above were a regular cat's cradle of warps from all the dinghies which had arrived before us, and we added ours to the general maelstrom.

There was a real party atmosphere in town; colourful bunting and rows of flags were festooning all the buildings and lots of the really big yachts were 'dressed overall'.

Our first call was at the famous "Mish Mish" hotel to try and book a table for dinner. They were of course madly busy, but would be able to fit us in at 9pm. The next thing was to try and get a bath; this wasn't so easy as there was great demand and we would have to wait until 11am in the morning when we might be lucky.

Whilst waiting for dinner, we sampled the ale at several of the other pubs in the town, and were in a very relaxed and jovial mood when we eventually sat down for our meal. The food in Scotland is usually good and served in generous helpings, and we were not disappointed.

Later in the evening, when we walked along to the McBrain Quay, we found that the Town Band had just arrived; strings of coloured lights were switched on, and suddenly everyone was dancing. We were very happy to join in the fun and Sheila took it in turns to dance with the men. The revelries went on until 1am, and finished up with a firework display. We were glad our boat was the other side of the harbour, as quite a few of the rockets seemed to be landing in the water.

When the time to return to our boat arrived, and we went to find the dinghy, it was missing. Oh dear! Panic – had it been stolen? And if so what were we to do? I made frantic enquiries of other skippers and it transpired that someone had noticed their dinghy being rowed away, and had "borrowed" our dinghy to chase them. Much to our relief it was returned a little later.

It so happened that August 2nd was Sheila's birthday and Philip disappeared into town in search of a present. He came back with a very nice silver-plated toast rack and an amusing tale.

Apparently the shop assistant was an ancient lady, and when he asked the price he was told that she "would have to refer him to a higher authority". The toast rack ever afterwards was known as "The higher authority toast rack".

Sam went to buy his wife a present, and came back with a gadget which, when inserted in a sauce bottle, would extract the last dregs. His wife had been a hospital Sister, and had been renowned for her efficiency.

We stayed for three days in Tobermory and thoroughly enjoyed ourselves by going for long walks in the beautiful country lanes which were ablaze with wild flowers.

All good things come to an end, and it was time to start on the long sail back to Beaumaris. We did it in easy one-night stands at Oban, Ghia, Girvan, Port Patrick and Port St Mary. We were fortunate in having a good steady reaching wind for most of the way until we go to the Isle of Man, when we suddenly became becalmed and had to motor sail for the final leg home.

This was the forerunner to many sails up to Scotland in *Magic Dragon* over the years, in many of which we had the companionship of the Venturers. We sailed into practically every loch in Scotland and to the isles of Eigg, Rhum, Canna and Skye. One year we landed on the Outer Hebrides.

CHAPTER 13

FIDDLER OF ORWELL'

MAGIC DRAGON had been an excellent boat; she was a single keeler and proved to be both fast and comfortable. When we cruised with the fleet, we were invariably amongst the first to arrive at our destination.

In the course of our cruising I had been very impressed by the outstanding performance and beautiful lines of a Hustler 35, and it wasn't long before I decided that I must have one. The Hustler was one of the big tough offshore types of boat that used to take part in the Fastnet Races. She had a two-ton lead keel, six excellent berths, a full size chart table and a wonderful feeling of stability. After a lot of searching, I eventually bought *Fiddler of Orwell*.

She was ashore at Emsworth Harbour and needed a number of minor repairs and modifications before she could be launched. I persuaded my old friend Tony Stromberg to accompany us down to Emsworth and carry out the necessary work. Tony had owned an engineering works before he retired and was a brilliant engineer as well as a sailor. He had an ancient Dormobile which he intended sleeping in, so we all piled in to that and made our way down south.

After a week of hard work, renewing various rigging, re-wiring some of the instruments, fitting an electric anchor winch, anti-fouling, and so on, we were eventually ready for launching.

Unfortunately Tony had a previous engagement and had to get back home, so Sheila and I had the daunting job of taking off in a very powerful untried boat, which if racing normally had a crew of at least six.

The previous owner Tom Cole offered to accompany us on the

"Fiddler of Orwell".

short sail across to Cowes, in order to show us how all the halyards and winches worked but after that we would be on our own..

Cowes is a world-renowned place of glamour, and is usually overflowing with hundreds of beautiful yachts. The snag is that all the medium-sized ones have to raft up against each other, so that when you go to bed you can be awoken at 2:00am by dozens of merry sailor boys scampering across your deck in order to reach their own boat, which could be in a row of seven.

We didn't get much sleep that night and were glad to see the dawn.

The time of the year was late May; there was a sharp nip in the air and a good brisk breeze as we started the Volvo engine and crept out of our berth at 7:00am the next day.

Once we were out of the harbour I headed the boat into the wind, handed the helm to Sheila and hoisted the mainsail. Our destination was Weymouth, but we thought we would probably have to put in somewhere on the way. Our mast head flag indicated that the wind was almost directly ahead so it was going to be a beat all the way, which is the most tiring point of sailing.

The weather forecast was not encouraging and indicated that the wind would increase, so I only clipped on our No 3 Genoa. My choice proved to be right, as after two hours' sailing we were belting into a Force 6 with the decks awash and the gunwale in the water. By this time I was dying for a pee but daren't let go of the helm, as in these conditions and with tiller steering, after being used to the Moody's wheel, Sheila didn't feel competent to take over.

A bailer was quickly unearthed, much to my relief.

Sheila was not happy beating in to this heavy sea, and wanted me to put in to Lymington for the night. I was thoroughly enjoying myself with the feeling of power which the heavy keel gave to the boat, and she felt perfectly safe; I could however appreciate my wife's apprehension, as the boat was new to us and she had probably not gelled with it quite as much as I had .

We were by now going at a great rate of knots and would shortly be off The Needles and into more open water where we could expect an even rougher sea, so I decided that it would probably be best to put in to Yarmouth on the Isle of Wight for the night.

When we reached there we found that we would have to moor up amongst a battery of piles (large upright pieces of wood which have been driven in to the mud). This was something which we had not encountered before, so we lowered our sails, started the engine and motored in. It was quite tricky for two people as it was necessary to tie up both fore and aft between two piles and also not come into contact with any other boat. It was made doubly difficult as our engine decided to cut out at the crucial moment and then refused to re-start.

This was serious as we certainly wouldn't be able to extricate ourselves from the piles in the morning without the engine. I went ashore and made enquiries to find out if there was a garage in the vicinity; it transpired that there was one just down the road so I went down there and managed to get a mechanic to come back to the boat with his diagnostic equipment. His tests indicated that we had a faulty battery, so he returned back to the garage, came back and fitted a new one which cost £87. My thoughts on the previous owner were unprintable.

The weather forecast for the next day was much better, so we had a cup of tea, extricated ourselves from the piles and were on our way to Weymouth by 7:30am. We could have breakfast on the way.

The day broke with brilliant sunshine, and the wind had abated to Force 3-4 on the beam so we had a broad reach for most of the way. We attached the self-steering and just lay back in the cockpit letting the boat sail herself. Sheila forgave me for changing from *Magic Dragon* when she saw how fast and seaworthy *Fiddler* was.

At the beginning of the afternoon, just after lunch, the wind died so we had to start the engine; we motored for three hours and suddenly the engine started to overheat so we had to cut it and hoist the sails once again. By this time the wind had freshened, so I used our enormous No 1 Genoa and we rolled along at a respectable 7 knots. We had two racing spinnakers, but when I looked at the two great big booming out spars and thought of Sheila on the helm I decided to give it a miss and wait until we had extra hands.

We arrived in Weymouth Bay in the early evening and tied up along the quayside. After an hour the Harbourmaster came along and directed us to a more permanent berth as I told him we would be staying for a week

Our son Richard, who is crazy about sailing and had been crewing on a Hustler 35 for a year in Irish Sea Racing, was of course dying to get his hands on *Fiddler* so it had been arranged that he, his wife Anne, and their two little daughters Kate and Nicky (who was only two years old) would motor down to Weymouth and join us on board. We would all sail over to Alderney, then to Cherbourg and finally to St Peter Port, on the Isle of Wight.

We had nearly a week before they arrived , so we busied ourselves provisioning the boat for six people and enjoyed ourselves exploring the town. We also had an engineer on board to sort out the engine overheat.

We had a super position in the harbour and were very fortunate that the annual regatta was to be held that week. When the great day arrived we had a bird's eye view of all the proceedings, which included a fishing boat race around the outer harbour, swimming races and water cannon fights between several naval vessels.

CHAPTER 14

GUESTS ON BOARD

WHEN RICHARD AND Anne arrived they deposited on the quayside about 20 bags filled with blankets, packets of baby's nappies, piles of sailing gear, food, etc, etc. Where on earth was it all going to go? Richard obviously knew his Hustler, and in no time at all had it all safely stowed away. I was amazed at how well the accommodation had been planned. That night we decided to go for a short cruise outside the harbour so that they could get the feel of the boat, before we set off for Cherbourg the next day. Everyone settled in their bunks very well and had a good night's sleep.

It was decided that the best plan would be to do our sailing overnight when the children would be asleep, so we crept out of the harbour at about midnight. It was a pitch black night, so having plotted our course and allowed for tide and currents we settled down in the shelter of the cockpit. We could of course of taken watches, but nobody felt sleepy. We were lucky there was a moderate breeze and we were on a broad reach all the way.

We arrived in Cherbourg in the early hours, found a berth in the harbour and waited until the children were awake; we then wandered into town, found a nice little restaurant and ordered breakfast which included some freshly baked *croissants*.

We spent the day sightseeing and then wearily trooped back to the boat for dinner. *Fiddler* had a first class galley and under Sheila's direction we always had the usual pre-dinner drinks followed by soup, main course and sweet, all washed down with a good bottle of wine. So we didn't starve our crews.

Next morning we were off bright and early for Alderney, which was on our way to Guernsey. This time it was a brisk beat followed

In Cherbourg harbour.

by a close reach. We got to Alderney about mid morning, and as we only wanted to spend the one day there, we decided to hire a car so that we could see as much as possible of the island in the time available. It is a lovely little island, and the country lanes were a delight; we wished that we could have spent more time there but Richard's stay was limited. We would have liked to have had dinner ashore, but had the children to consider. Still – I don't suppose we would have fared any better.

Guernsey – here we come. When we arrived it was low water, so we had to take our turn and wait in the outer harbour at St Peter Port until the tide rose sufficiently to allow us to enter the inner harbour, where you can tie up along the pontoon. Whilst we were there we became friendly with a German couple; they were obviously fanatics as their boat shone as if it had never been in the water and they even had a piece of red carpet to wipe your feet on before you entered the cockpit. They invited Sheila and me for dinner; which we accepted with trepidation. We were given drinks in cut glass wineglasses, and the *cordon bleu* dinner was served on china plates with silver-plated cutlery. A coloured glass lamp adorned the table. Apparently all this gear was carefully wrapped up and stowed in cardboard boxes before they set sail.

We stayed two nights in Guernsey, then returned to Weymouth.

CHAPTER 15

HOMEWARD BOUND

ONCE BACK AT Weymouth, we helped Richard and Anne to remove all their gear from the boat and load it back into their car. Richard was very loath to say goodbye to *Fiddler*, but I promised him that he would have many more opportunities for a sail when we got her back home. He is an expert crew, and with his youth and brawn made light work of setting those hefty spinnaker poles when later on we took her racing.

Our time at Weymouth was now up and so the next thing was to prepare for the long sail back to Beaumaris. We had two volunteers as crew to assist us. One was Tom Cole, the previous owner (we had forgiven him the dud battery) and the other was Dr John Bennett – a respected member of the Venturers and an experienced navigator who owned *Avignon*, a 36ft deep keeler. We had arranged to pick them up at Falmouth in four days' time, so we got our charts out that evening and plotted our course. Just after leaving Dartmouth we had to round Portland Bill, a renowned spot for dangerous tidal currents, so we thought we would have a walk along the cliffs to the lighthouse and see the best line to take. It was a lovely sunny evening without a breath of wind and down below the water looked like a millpond, but we could see from the gently swirling motion that in a blow it could be very different.

Fortunately the weather next day was very similar and as there was no wind we motored around The Bill.

Mid-morning the wind picked up to a gentle Force 3 so I hoisted the No 1 Genoa and the mainsail, set the self-steering and let her sail herself. By 5:00pm we were entering Falmouth Harbour. We sailed down towards the yacht club and picked up a mooring. We hadn't been there long before the Harbourmaster's launch came alongside and we got permission to stay for a couple of nights. I inflated our dinghy and we went ashore to the Yacht Club for a drink. I made enquiries and found that we could order dinner for a little time later, so we did, and then went for a walk to stretch our 'sea legs'.

The next day, as we were not in a desperate hurry, we had an enjoyable cruise up the river and were delighted to see, and try to identify, all the many species of birds that came down to feed. Sheila cooked one of her special dinners, we split a bottle of Chasse du Pape, relaxed, and had an early night.

Tom and John arrived the next morning and we went ashore in the dinghy to pick them up.

John could only manage to stay for three days, so we would have to make a fast non-stop passage home. We had a quick meal, slipped our mooring and were away.

It was slightly foggy when we left harbour and Sheila and I were a little apprehensive, however our two expert navigators didn't seem perturbed. There was no wind so we motored all the way past Land's End, by which time the fog had become more dense. We consulted as to what course to take and it was decided that as we were not in a dense shipping lane we would sail a direct course due North, hoping that the fog would lift and we would be able to sail. It was of course necessary to have one of the crew on constant watch, and trust in our radar reflector.

By 7:00am the fog began to lift and we felt a gentle breeze, so we hoisted the sails. We had taken watches, but under the circumstances nobody had had much sleep.

By 9:00am we were bowling along with a steady Force 5 on the beam. Sheila cooked us all a huge breakfast of bacon and eggs, and we all began to relax.

Now that we felt out of danger we set a four-hour watch, which the men did, and we continued on our marathon sail

By mid-day of the third day, we were approaching Caernarfon Bar, which is well buoyed but in a real blow can be a terrifying place to be; we were lucky as it was half tide and the wind had dropped to a Force 2. Unfortunately we would be on an adverse tide if we attempted to go through the Swellies, so we decided to wait until the morning, stay the night in Caernarfon, go ashore, and have dinner. I am afraid John was slightly late in arriving, but in sailing it's impossible to be precise.

It felt great to be home and have my dream boat safely on her mooring outside our cottage, where I could keep an eye on her. Many thanks to John and Tom for an exciting delivery sail!

CHAPTER 16

CARAVANNING

WHAT DO YOU do when you can no longer sail? (Commit suicide! Well, some people have.) Why, of course you look for new hobbies and ways of getting around, and the nearest thing to sailing would be caravanning; not the static type but something highly mobile.

We had in the past owned two motor caravans, a new Volkswagen Auto Sleeper and a new Ford Auto Sleeper.

There are advantages and disadvantages in motor caravans. The Volkswagen had a very comfortable ride, but it had rear-wheel drive, was very light on the front and could be really scary if you got caught in a strong cross-wind. It also had a cumbersome double bed sleeping arrangement which occupied the entire rear portion of the van and the only exit was through a sliding door. Very neighbourly if you wanted a pee in the middle of the night. We only kept it for one year.

The Ford Auto Sleeper was much better: it had a centre passage with a berth on each side, and it also had plenty of power and much better road-holding. We kept that one for four years.

The advantage of a motor caravan is that it is instantly ready for action and is much easier to park and manoeuvre on site than a trailer; against that it has a number of disadvantages. If you intend to stay somewhere for any length of time, then it has to be positioned on a very level piece of ground; it can be chocked up with wedges, or even jacked up fore and aft, but every time you want to go anywhere you have got to repeat the procedure, and in addition you have also got to disconnect the drainage barrel and the electric hook-up, etc. Trailers are much easier, as they have wind-down jacks at each corner.

When we retired from sailing, we decided that if we were going to do more caravanning it would have to be in more comfort.

Our first trailer van was a year-old 14ft Swift Corniche, which was in new condition. At that time my main car was a 2-litre automatic Honda Estate which I had to have fitted with a towbar and all the necessary electrical connections plus special extending driving mirrors

One of the first things to do before starting any serious caravanning is to join The Caravan Club. This gives you access to all the best sites throughout the country; the club provides you with a book and map with full details of cost, access roads, and all sorts of useful information.

When trailing a van, if you have not had any previous experience, its advisable to take it to large field and practice reversing into a marked-out space. It's not as easy as it looks, and when you arrive on a site where all the occupants are safely parked and sitting in their deck chairs, you will save yourself from becoming a victim of mirth. The next thing, and believe you me this is most important, try and have a planned route with any possible hazards marked out. This is particularly important when you are approaching your booked site, as you will be leaving the main road and getting on to narrow lanes and even single no-passing places. Look well ahead to see that you are not going to meet another van leaving the site. Or you might be glad of my practice field advice if you had to reverse for 500yds...

That is the only real disadvantage of a trailer van, but you will certainly have a much more comfortable holiday.

The 14ft Corniche was most enjoyable and towed superbly behind my Honda; we enjoyed it so much that we ordered one of the very latest 15ft models for delivery in May the following year. This one really was the last word in luxury as it had a large end bathroom with central heating, double glazing, fly screens, a flushing sealed toilet unit and a built-in television and CD unit.

We had taken the 14ft van on a number of short trips; including a week at Criccieth on a small private site by the side of the river.

One of the advantages of the caravan was that we could take Judy, our golden retriever, with us. She wasn't too keen on the journey, as she had to be confined to the back of the car, but she loved it when we arrived on the site and we were able to take her on lovely walks across the fields. Of course she had a swim in the river, too. She made the back of the estate her home, so that she was certain that she wasn't going to be left behind.

As I mentioned, it was the beginning of May when we got our new van and so we decided to take it for a long haul up to the Lake District, in the hope of getting the best of the spring sunshine and avoiding the build-up of traffic which would be unavoidable later in the year. Our destination was Lake Coniston.

The Isle of Anglesey, where we live, is a bit 'out on a leg' before you start to get anywhere and the first part of the journey around the Queen's Ferry area can be a nightmare if you get involved with traffic going to work in Manchester.

We set off at 6am and were well on our way before the rest of the world was awake. Once clear of Preston I almost forgot that I was 'being followed'. I had been in touch with The Caravan Club and they advised an overnight stop at Overton, so we had booked a place there for the night. We had one or two breaks on the way and it was early afternoon when we arrived.

The site wasn't far off the main road, so it was the ideal place for a short stop. They had a small café, so we had a reasonable meal there, took Judy for a short walk, and retired to bed early, being somewhat sleepy after our early morning start.

The next day we had a leisurely breakfast, and then had an unhurried run up to Coniston.

We found Park Coppice Caravan Club Site to be first class. It was situated 400yds from the lakeside and we had no difficulty in finding a super position, facing south, and with a view of the lake.

There was a small shop which sold most of our basic requirements and an excellent toilet block with hot showers, shaving points, etc. Our new van was so comfortable and warm that we mostly showered 'at home'.

We were lucky, and had struck a period with nice sunny days, although the nights were somewhat chilly.

When Judy saw the lake she started wagging her tail and we hadn't the heart to stop her plunging in. The only snag is that Golden Retrievers, with their long coats, take an awful lot of drying, and it took three towels before she was fit to sit in her favourite place in the caravan.

Coniston is a beautiful lake and is surrounded by magnificent scenery, so we got our walking boots out and each day she joined us on our trails.

I had just recently bought a super pair of Cannon 12 magnification stabilised binoculars, so was looking forward to trying them out on the teeming bird life, The more normal magnification for bird watching is 8 which gives a good wide field of view; but if you really want to identify a bird you need a 12. The trouble is a 12 is almost impossible to hold steady without using a cumbersome tripod. The latest stabilised Cannon has an electronic system, which produces a crystal clear steady image.

We were lucky to identify 15 different species, and on one day even saw an Osprey swooping down to make its kill. We are members of the RSPB, so we sent them a list of our sightings.

A drive to Coniston would not be complete without a visit to the World of Beatrix Potter, the famous author of the wonderful animal stories which we cherished in our childhood. Her cottage has of course been considerably updated; and Peter Rabbit, Jemima Puddleduck and all the other famous characters are really lifelike. We felt very nostalgic.

William Wordsworth, the famous poet, is another local celebrity and was educated at the Grammar School at Hawkshead. We went to see Dove Cottage, his first home after he married his childhood sweetheart Mary Hutchinson; their first three children were born there. We also visited Rydal Mount, which was their final home, where they remained until their deaths. It is on a superb site overlooking the lake; we had to take it in turns to view the interior,

Judy loved coming with us for caravan trips.

with its masses of memorabilia, because of Judy, but she was very well trained and no trouble at all when she joined us later for a cream tea on the terrace, and a walk around the superb garden.

Whilst we were having our tea a little Robin came and adopted us. He was so tame that he sat on my plate and devoured the crumbs as fast as I could feed him.

We spent a fortnight in Coniston and district and enjoyed every minute of it.

On the way home we decided to break the journey at Wigan, and park for the night. Being sailors we had heard a lot of jokes about Wigan Pier, so we decided to investigate.

There is indeed a little pier which overlooks the canal. There is also a superb bar and restaurant, which supplied us with a most excellent dinner. Pleasure trips are run up and down the canal in a *bateau mouche*.

The main attraction there is an absolutely spectacular museum which depicts a bye-gone age, from Victorian times to the present day.

It is set in a huge old warehouse, with a series of lifelike figures all going about their jobs as they did many years ago. Everything is authentic; old pubs lit by gaslight, with all the original bars, beer pumps, and barmaids in authentic period dresses. A dentist in a primitive surgery extracts a tooth from an unwilling victim. A working blacksmith's shop has sparks flying from the forge. There is part of an old railway station, with its booking office and cashier stamping out tickets in one of the original machines. Stuffed donkeys give children rides on the seashore and there are Penny Farthing bicycles complete with rider.

These are but a few of the hundreds of lifelike exhibits; but the highlight of the exhibition was a recreation of a village school as things used to be at the beginning of the 20th century.

An actress had been employed and she was wearing an ankle-length dark blue dress of the period, together with a high neck white blouse. Her hair was 'rouched' up with a large black bow at the back and in her hand she carried a thin cane.

A show was given every hour, and she stood at the entrance to the classroom directing the audience (children) in, "Boys to the left, girls to the right." It was a replica of a classroom, complete with blackboard and school desks.

When all the 'pupils' were seated she proceeded to start a lesson.

"Now, I am not going to repeat this; if there is any talking or lack of attention I shall deal with it most severely. That boy on the third row with a blue shirt, stop picking your nose immediately and pay attention!"

She then went on to give a short talk about the Royal Family, and then started asking questions on what she had been talking about.

"You girl, on the fifth row, wearing a pink jumper! What is your name?"

"Please miss, it's Jessie."

"Jessie, how old was Queen Elizabeth II when she came to the throne? No, she was not 80! Report to me after class. The girl on the second row wearing earrings! Come to the front of the class.

Good gracious, you are also wearing lipstick… (this happened to be Sheila) …what is your name?"

"Sheila. Please miss, me mum said the earrings would make me see better," she replied.

It was a hilarious lesson, and greatly enjoyed by all the 'pupils'.

Interestingly on the other side of the motorway going home there is a place called Orrell. This was reputedly named after my ancestors who originated from the area – the derivation of the name being "Ore Hill". It is now of course the home of a famous rugby football club.

We had many pleasurable holidays in the caravan: a complete tour of the Scottish Highlands re-visiting many of our old sailing haunts, several trips down to Devon and Cornwall, a visit to Newquay in Wales and several visits to Tewkesbury to tour the delightful surrounding countryside.

When I passed 86 years old, Sheila decided that we had had enough of caravanning. I think it was the fear of meeting another van on a very narrow lane that eventually got to her; anyway she persuaded me that I was now too old to be kneeling down in the rain to remove heavy wheel clamps, something which was occasionally necessary when it was time to go home. I must admit the water barrels and waste disposal units were getting a bit heavier. Much to my regret we sold our beautiful van.

One thing I missed was the relaxed atmosphere for painting. We have been painting now for about 20 years and thoroughly enjoy it. On days when we inevitably had rain we used to get our paints out, put a tape on and settle down comfortably to paint. We now go on holiday and stay in hotels, and find it much more of an effort to get started.

Sheila's answer to that was to arrange for us to go on a fortnight's painting holiday down at Rod William's Studio in St Davids, in order to get us painting seriously once again. No matter how long you have been painting, even the experts like to have a refresher course to get back to the basics.

Rod Williams is a well-respected professional and his painting holidays are much in demand. His studio is situated in a large three-storey Victorian house in the centre of St Davids and the courses are programmed to cater for six people.

The house has a pleasant lounge, which is filled with lots of expensive books on art; these are freely available for study. The dining room – where the students are served their breakfast and evening meal – has a large circular table so is an ideal spot to discuss the day's paintings with the other inmates.

Each morning at 9:30am Rod drove his luxury seven-seater Toyota Previa to the front door and loaded our painting gear in to the specially partitioned rear compartment, not forgetting seven delicious packed lunches. It was then 'all aboard' and we were off for the day to a spot chosen by Rod for its scenic beauty, where we would set up our easels and try to produce a masterpiece. About every 40 minutes Rod came around and offered his help and advice. At 12:30pm we all met for a chat and communal lunch. At 4:30pm all our paintings were safely stowed away and we were then driven back to base. A cup of tea and biscuits was provided, and we were then free until the 7:00pm dinner.

Rod has a super studio, which occupies the whole of the third floor. It has special roof lights and is equipped with custom-built desks and easels, a projector, a hot drinks machine, and a plentiful supply of paints and brushes which you can purchase if you run short.

After the evening meal the studio was available for anyone who wished to go up there and touch up his or her paintings. Every other night Rod gave us a talk, sometimes illustrated by slides.

On the last day of the course we displayed all the paintings we had produced and he gave his expert criticism and suggestions. It was all very light-hearted and nobody was ridiculed or embarrassed.

At that time both Sheila and myself were working in oils so we didn't produce quite as many paintings as the other four who were doing watercolours, which dry a lot faster, On the odd day when it rained, we were taken to view various local art exhibitions and given an expert appraisal. The holiday was most enjoyable and we came away with much useful advice and a number of saleable pictures. Now that we are older, and not quite as active, we do find that our painting is a great comfort to us.

We have been members of The Straits Art Society and the Anglesey Art Society for many years. We meet up with our friends once a fortnight and paint together, under the present guidance of Chris Hull who was a finalist in the recent television painting competition. For many years we had the benefit of Jeremy Yates who is well-known for his outstanding exhibitions.

Every year the societies have their own exhibitions in Beaumaris and over the years we have been lucky enough to sell a number of our pictures. You won't make a fortune in your lifetime, but there you are. It's reputed that Van Gogh never sold a picture whilst he was alive. It's very rewarding to find that some stranger will pay good money for your picture, albeit not as much as you think it's worth!

CHAPTER 17

GARDENING - AND THE FAMILY

I DON'T THINK I have mentioned very much about our garden, so I'll put that right now.

On 2nd June, 2005 I celebrated my 90th birthday with a party for 54 of my closest friends and, of course, the family. We did wonder whether to have it in one of the local hotels but the family decided that it would be better to have caterers in and have it at home.

It seemed a pity to confine our guests to some stuffy hotel in the middle of the summer, when we have a superb garden with magnificent views.

As you know, we live right down on the banks of the Menai Straits with views across to Penmaenmawr, The Great Orme, and Puffin Island.

When we first bought Minnows 25 years ago there were no trees and the land, which is about an acre, was just a wilderness. Over the years we planted 15 apple and pear trees and surrounded the property with rose and Escalonia hedges.

The main theme has been to concentrate on Heathers, Azaleas, Brooms and Hydrangeas, plus a very large herbaceous border which was designed by Sheila.

When I was 80, I decided to build a fish pond 20ft long, 8ft wide and 3ft deep; I dug it out myself in a fortnight, lined it with old carpet, and then a butyl lining. I did think of filling it with Koi, but they are very expensive, and can be a lot of trouble; also, as we have a resident heron on the beach they probably wouldn't have lived very long, so I bought Golden Orfe and Goldfish. When it was established I fitted a Henri cascading water statue. A year later I got my old friend Ken Thomas to build another pond with

When I was 80 I dug
out a 20ft-long fish
pond, then lined it with
old carpet and a butyl
lining.

Busy creating a raised flowerbed in the garden, to stand near the new pond.

a waterfall. Two years later we managed to get Bob Duff, a local character, to build us a wildlife pond 30ft long which trailed off into a bog garden. Bob really is a master plumber but is also expert on all sorts of other things and immensely strong. I ordered two lorry-loads of stone from the quarry at Moelfre, and in the course of four days he designed and made a super rock garden with a natural stone water feature in the centre. A little later we had a large summer house built and positioned between the two ponds, so that we have a perfect view of all the wild creatures that come there to drink.

We are fortunate in having the help of Merfyn Roberts, our gardener, who comes and takes on some of the heavy lifting jobs which are now too much for me. Merfyn is a treasure – he is always cheerful and nothing is too much trouble for him.

And what about the family? Our younger daughter Jane is now a well established designer of superb wedding gowns and has regular shows around the Island. She and her husband Roger, who is a chartered surveyor, and our two grandchildren, Freyja and Calvin, are always popping in to see us. They are mad keen on amateur dramatics and we frequently have the pleasure of attending some of their productions. Our elder daughter Anne is resident in Calgary, Alberta; she emigrated at the age of 21 (and nearly broke my heart). She is happily married to a Canadian who is a chemical engineer, and they have three children, Brett, Kyla and Amber. Kyla has recently presented us with our second great-grandchild. Anne has just recently returned to Canada after her yearly visit to Anglesey.

Richard, our son, as I have mentioned, is in practice in New Brighton. He and his wife Anne, who is a teacher, live at Thornton Hough on the Wirral. They have a holiday home at Abersoch which they go to most weekends, so as they are on the way home they often break their journey and call in to see that we are OK. They have two children, our granddaughters, Kate and Nicky.

CHAPTER 18

CARS AND CATS

WHEN I REACHED the age of 90, and Sheila 88, we found that we were no longer able to undertake the long walks which used to give us so much pleasure.

Sheila's eyes were beginning to give her some trouble. She was developing the first symptoms of cataract, so although she was perfectly legal to drive, she was confining herself to local runs. So that she could have her last 'fling' I bought her a new silver blue Ford Focus for her birthday. Extraordinary coincidence, when I went to insure it I found that the registration number included my initials 'JEO'.

The Focus has proved to be a great little car, and handles even better than the Mondeo; we shall use it on all the shorter journeys, and my 2-litre Mondeo for holidays and longer trips.

If you have read my first book *It's Muck You Want*, you will know that over the years I have owned a number of glamorous cars but I must admit that ignoring the status angle (which no longer troubles me) I find the Mondeo an excellent car for modern conditions. It's spacious, fast, safe, comfortable and economical with a £100 a year service bill instead of the £700 which my Mercedes used to cost.

We have in the past owned a succession of dogs, including Pekingese, Cocker Spaniels, a Dachshund, Staffordshire Bull Terriers and Golden Retrievers

When Judy our Golden Retriever died at the age of 12, we were so upset that we said we would never have another dog. Eight years later and being more housebound, we began to feel that the house seemed empty without some energetic young creature running around.

I had a yen for a Cavalier King Charles, and started to scan all the local papers and the Internet for possible contacts.

Amazingly, all our children shouted me down. They argued, "You are both too old to have another dog. A dog would be a lot of work – you will have to groom it and you won't be able to give it the exercise it needs. We think it would be much better if you got a cat; they are no trouble, and look after themselves."

Eventually we had to admit defeat, and the hunt for a cat began.

We used to have five cats when we were on the farm, but they were working cats whose job it was to keep down the rats and mice. They lived outside in the barns and shippen, and never came in the house.

We decided that if we were going to have cats we would be better to have two as they would play together and be company for each other; we also wanted kittens, as they are so adorable when they are growing up.

I borrowed a book about cats from the library. It was full of pictures of all sorts of exotic breeds and I rather fancied getting a couple of Burmese kittens, but Sheila thought that at £400 each they would be a constant source of worry in case they got stolen, and that they would be more delicate than a 'moggie'.

Cats seem to have had a very chequered existence. The Egyptians worshipped them, and had their famous temple cats. Anyone found ill-treating a cat was put to death. On the other hand at one time in Ypres, Belgium they held a yearly ceremony, involving witchcraft in which cats were hurled from the top of their temples; amazingly most of them use to walk away, apparently unharmed. This ceremony apparently still takes place, but they now use toy cats. There are records of cats falling from New York skyscrapers and being alive.

Did you know that wherever a cat falls from it always lands on its feet?

In our quest for kittens, we first of all tried the local pet shop, which has a notice board advertising unwanted pets. There were plenty of stray dogs and mature cats but no kittens.

The next thing of course was the local paper, where we discovered a notice from an animal rescue home, saying that they had cats and kittens wanting a home. I rang them, explained our need, and made an appointment to go and see what was available. When we arrived in the vicinity of the home it started to pour with rain, and I had to lift a great heavy metal gate, which was set in a sea of mud, in order to gain access to a field which led up a muddy path to a hill and down a steep bank to another metal gate set in six inches of mud; this led into a farmyard in which there was a small house and a couple of wooden sheds. After a while a girl appeared and took us along to one of the sheds, which was divided into a number of cubicles, which housed a number of adult cats.

"They are all very nice, but we don't want an adult cat. As I told you on the phone; we want a couple of kittens!" I said.

"Oh, then you will have to see ….."

She disappeared into the house, and in a few minutes a wild-looking woman appeared, and shouted at us at the top of her voice: "It's no use, under no circumstances will I let you have any of my kittens; you are far too old. It's no use, my mind is made up and I won't change it."

We were really upset by the ferocity of her attack, which was entirely uncalled for. We beat a hasty retreat back through the mud and left her with all her kittens.

Next, we rang the RSPCA at Colwyn Bay and arranged to go and see what they had on offer.

On the day of our visit, it once again was pouring with rain and blowing a gale; however as we had made the appointment we decided to go. It was a difficult place to find, but when we arrived there we were very impressed by the spotless premises. Before we were allowed to inspect the kittens we were warned that at our age we were taking a great risk of being tripped up by a couple of active kittens; however it was a much kindlier approach, and on assuring them that we were very used to dealing with animals, and were prepared to take the risk, they relented somewhat.

We had assumed that we would be inundated with people offering unwanted kittens, but it wasn't that easy. They wanted to inspect our house to see if it was suitable, and wanted the particulars of who would re-house the kittens when we went to the Great Unknown. They had also got to have microchip identification put in their ears, have two injections and be neutered and wormed. I should hate to try and adopt a baby!

This was an entirely different approach to our other experience, and I think they are doing a great job.

The animals are housed in a brick built centrally heated premises, with a central passage down which there are a number of glass fronted cubicles each of which has an outdoor run.

There were a number of adult cats, but also several cubicles with different age litters. The one which caught my eye had a litter of five beautiful black and ginger tortoiseshells and one ginger. The ginger kitten had already been promised.

They were eight weeks old and we were allowed to take our choice. I plumped for one which has a white chest, whilst Sheila's has white above its eyes. They are both girls; their mother had apparently been sent in by her owner before the confinement, and had just returned home.

Our journey home was anything but pleasant; it rained so hard the whole way back that I could hardly see the road. When we reached Beaumaris we found the centre of the town was flooded, and the coastal road to our house completely impassable. We had no alternative but to book in for the night at the Bulkeley Arms which was the only hotel in the town which was not flooded. At £120 for the night it doubled the cost of our kittens; the chef had retired home and our evening meal consisted of a ham sandwich!

We had already decided on the names of the kittens; mine is Cleo and Sheila's is Pippa.. The next week we went and collected the two little 'bundles of fun'.

We were aware that we would have to be very careful not to be tripped up by them whilst they were so small, so to begin with I

Clio and Pippa

The punchline on this 90th birthday card from Jane reads: "Keep acting cute but as soon as they're not looking you claw the curtains and I'll crap in the laundry basket!" ("Virtual Search" by Phillip Parr, Emotional Rescue Ltd).

bought a piece of hardboard 3ft high and slotted it into the doorway between our kitchen and the utility room. Whilst any cooking was going on they were confined in the utility room to play with a Carousel type toy which I had made them.

It was amazing to see how quickly they grew, and we got tremendous pleasure in joining in their fun and games. It wasn't long before they scaled my barrier and I had to add another piece. They were litter-trained from the very start and soon had the run of the house.

I wouldn't recommend kittens to anyone who is house-proud. Fortunately most of the chairs in our lounge have loose covers which will all have to be replaced when the kittens get older and more sedate, as in their games of hide and seek they have covered them in claw marks. They have been lovely to watch, and we both adore them.

They are now a year old and are beginning to calm down. We have had a magnetic cat flap fitted in the glass panel of the utility room door, so they each have a magnetic collar which allows them to move in and out as they please, The only snag is they will keep bringing us in 'presents' of live mice and frogs which I have to rescue...

CHAPTER 19

AROUND THE ISLAND - MARCH 1973

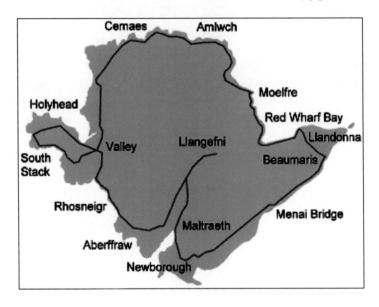

ABOUT A MONTH ago [March 1973] we spent a weekend at the cottage in Beaumaris, *writes Sheila*.

The weather was wet and dull, but we decided to go for a good walk and ignore the elements. We thought it would be interesting to walk across the nature reserve near Newborough and along the shore and round the corner of the island to Foel Ferry. We donned waterproofs and set off. We failed to reach Foel because of numerous tidal inlets and marshes, so had to return by the same route. We had of course mislaid our map at the outset. However, we so enjoyed ourselves that Jack made the fateful remark that it would be very pleasant to walk right round the coast of Anglesey, with packs on our backs, stopping at hotels each night, and walking on the next day.

On Monday of this week Jack arrived home with some proper hiking boots – real leather and with gorgeous yellow laces. They looked magnificent but alas proved to be unwearable. On Tuesday he literally went to town and purchased some more proper hiking boots – real leather and with pink laces – which also looked super and felt super. He also bought two red rucksacks and sundry pairs of socks, etc. On Wednesday I changed the yellow-laced boots for some trousers, more socks, a mess-kit for two, and two ex-WD capes, which were rather heavy but only cost 75p each.

Friday March 2nd, 1973

It took at least two hours to pack the rucksacks. Jack has two side pockets strapped on to his rucksack, and it was found essential that these should weigh approximately the same. We decided to take the small Gaz stove and the quart flask, to be used for coffee when available, or water, should we decide to cook up something ourselves.

We aimed at starting from home at 9:00am, and called in at Bangor to get some large-scale maps. We actually left at 9:30am but made good time, dumped the car at the cottage, ate some of our sandwiches with a cup of coffee, and finally started at 1:10pm to walk via Llandonna to Red Wharf Bay. Our packs felt terrible and I personally doubted whether I could walk to the end of the road. However, we pressed on and found that the hill up the Pentraeth road was a killer. There was a gale force wind that blew diagonally against us. We turned right at the top of the hill for Llandonna and found the wind even stronger, but occasionally with us, as the road wound round considerably. After turning the corner we checked the pedometer, which our friend Bill had kindly lent us. It hadn't even registered. However, after a bit of fiddling, we suspended it from the zip of Jack's pocket and it started to cooperate. We raised our packs

The start of the walk, with a well packed and extremely heavy rucksack.

slightly and began to feel more comfortable. The wind roared and the telegraph poles were shaking like mad. We tried to walk facing the traffic as it was impossible to hear any cars coming up behind us. We kept changing sides when we walked into sharp right-hand bends.

When we reached our first cross-roads either we went one mile to Llandonna or four miles to Pentraeth. We consulted the map; trying to get shelter behind a telephone box, we were almost tempted to go inside but the thought of the necessary de-packing deterred us. We continued to Llandonna. The other way did advertise an hotel, but we had only walked three miles! The pedometer and signpost were in agreement. I had not packed any sweets, so on reaching the village we were pleased to see the Post Office where we were able to buy some Everton mints and butterscotch. The postmistress directed us to turn left for the beach. She also said that there was an hotel on the far side of Red Wharf Bay, and provided that the tide was out, we could walk diagonally across the shore. If, however, the tide was coming in, she said that the river got quite deep, and although we wouldn't drown, we could be wading waist deep.

The road down to the beach was lovely; very narrow and winding. We passed some rather pretty modernized cottages, obviously used as holiday homes. In one row of gaily painted cottages we were surprised to see flowers in bloom in an upturned butter churn; we also passed some beautiful modern bungalows with superb views, and a partially-renovated cottage with four acres which was for sale.

The shore was bleak. The sun had been shining and the sea looked beautiful – really blue with lovely white horses – but visibility deteriorated. We came to a stream running across the sand. It was too deep for my shoes, so Jack took both packs across, and then came back and carried me. The wind blew off the land and the sand blew in clouds towards the sea. We plodded on towards the far side of the bay and soon came to another 'river' where we repeated the process. This happened several times, until I decided to paddle through. My despised non-leather shoes really were waterproof. Walking was really hard, with the sand blowing in our eyes and the wind making it difficult to keep our balance with our packs. The shore seemed enormous, but we did eventually feel that we had come at least half way. We noticed some dinghy masts way up on the left and we had a nasty suspicion that we had not yet crossed the 'river'. We were soon proved right, and found the river wider than the other streams, very fast flowing and quite deep. We walked upstream towards some stones, which turned out to

We stayed the first night at the Min-Y-Don hotel, where we enjoyed a much-appreciated hot bath and an excellent meal.

In the morning it was raining heavily and I put on my ex-WD cape.

be mussel shells. We considered wading barefoot, but the thought of the sharp shells deterred us. Jack suggested going downstream in the hope of finding the river shallower and more widespread. We walked almost to the tide line and Jack was just able to wade through in his boots. To have taken them off would have been a major operation. I had to take my shoes off and turn up my trousers. It was perhaps a mistake to wear tights. However, it couldn't be helped, and in I padded, tights and all. It was freezing. We walked to the shelter of the rocks before I put my shoes and socks on again. We saw a building which looked like an hotel. It was in fact the club attached to the caravan site. We enquired about accommodation and were directed to the Min-Y-Don Hotel. We managed to get a room, and had pot of tea in the lounge, where there was a fire and TV. There were also fires in the bar and dining room. We had much appreciated hot baths, and after an excellent meal, retired to bed.

Saturday, March 3rd, 1973

We spent a reasonable night in our tiny bedroom overlooking the bay. We had a door-key but couldn't use it as the door would not even close. We opened the window slightly and it rattled. Jack cured it with a couple of maps and a comb.

We got up at about 7:15am, and after much heart-searching decided to jettison some of our baggage. At the outset Jack had decided to bring his thin nylon mackintosh instead of his WD cape, as it weighed so much less. In actual fact we found that he had brought both. We decided to leave the stove and mess kit, two shirts, lots of underwear, a pair of trousers and my blouse, also the tins of soup, coffee, sugar, spare Gaz cylinder, and Jack's cape. It made us very sad to leave the stove as Jack had great longings to cook bacon *al fresco* and I was much enamored with our mess kit. I did extricate the two mugs as they are very light and easier to use than disposable ones. Our little waitress seemed quite happy to fill our flask with coffee, make us sandwiches for lunch and to keep watch over our excess baggage until next weekend. The fire was lit in the dining room for breakfast (it went out but was quickly revived with some white firelighters).

We finally got out at 10:00am. It was raining heavily and I donned my cape and Jack his mack. The tide was in, so we had to go via the cliff path. We took a few wrong turnings but eventually circumnavigated the castle rock and took to the shore. We proceeded partly by cliff paths and partly by the shore until we got down to Benllech, where we walked along the front. It was like a little ghost village with all the cafés closed and the houses also appeared deserted. We consulted our map and found that there was a path over the cliffs that wound around to Moelfre. This was beautiful.

The rain eased off and the sky grew lighter and we really felt that this was how we had envisaged walking round Anglesey. The path was narrow and extremely muddy, and we climbed up considerably from the beach. We had some anxious moments in places where there were gaps in the path, and the possibility of slipping down the sloping cliffs was rather obvious. We negotiated a few of these gaps on our backsides. Having the packs made it much more difficult; we were very hot so we stopped for coffee on a gentle grassy slope prior to tackling the rather steep path ahead, which went round the headland. We took off our waterproofs and I shed a sweater.

The path ahead was very overgrown, but at least there was plenty of scrub on the seaward side, which was rather comforting to know; the steep part was not so muddy. The sun now shone and the sea was so clear and blue. We had one very bad patch in the path, where there was a deep hollow sloping seawards. We crossed this by squatting down facing the sea and working sideways, We were now really muddied up. The path led inland, so we took off our packs and climbed down a steep and muddy slope to a lovely beach. We had more shore walking, then climbing over and down the rocks to the shore of Traeth Bychan. We were getting thirsty and hoped to find a pub or café, but there was no pub and the café was, of course, closed.

We were a little unsure how to proceed to Moelfre. It was either over the cliff path or over the rocks on the shore. We asked a man in a large house that looked like a pub, as there were several cars outside and a crate of milk – maybe it was a farmhouse. He directed us to a path across a field of cattle. This eventually became a public footpath and got wetter and muddier and smellier. I nearly lost my shoe several times, but my feet did remain dry.

We walked past a farm and many smells and eventually to Moelfre. It was after 1:30pm and we both thought that Jack deserved a pint. Would we make Moelfre before closing time? Jack called a halt and started pulling up handfuls of grass to clean his boots and thus render him fit to get into a pub. We both cleaned ourselves up and then proceeded downhill into lots more mud. Where was Moelfre, and where was the pub? There was Ann's Pantry and Ann's various other things.

I asked a woman with a child in the car park, who was real Lancashire, who said she "didn't *go* in them places herself," but directed us across the road to the pub, and suggested we go in the beach room which was uncarpeted and where they didn't mind mud. She seemed extremely well informed for a non-drinker. We entered the beach room and Jack got his pint and a pint of lemonade for me, and in due course some nice fresh beef sandwiches.

An amusing little man was very interested in us; eventually he gave us his name and address and asked us to send him a card if we managed to walk round the island. Jack took his photo standing outside the door, much to the amusement of his pals inside. He directed us to Amlwch via the road. He said it was about five miles, but it turned out to be nearer ten.

For a while the road ran parallel to the sea and was quite pleasant. We saw two tiny black twin lambs minus their mother. It worried me and I mentioned it to a man in a parked car, who assured me that the farmer would be along in a minute. We began to tire appreciably and stopped for another swig of our black, sugarless coffee and a Min-Y-Don sandwich. It began to rain slightly and grew very dull. We reckoned it was five miles to Amlwch from where we were.

We encountered more traffic as we had now arrived on the main road, although for much of the way there was a footpath. The rain got steadier and it became quite misty. One motorist stopped and offered us a lift to Amlwch, but we decided to make it unaided. We met a strange-looking man in the pouring rain, wearing neither coat nor jacket. We estimated another mile to Amlwch, but he said two or nearer three, which was very depressing.

We finally reached a roundabout and a garage where we got further directions. We soon arrived in the town and located the Dinorben Arms. It was very nice and warm. I suggested a pot of tea, but the beautiful young man who received us said there was no staff until 6pm. I felt that he might have managed it himself as we were the only residents. Meanwhile we lay on the bed and relaxed. At 6:05pm there was a knock on the door and a pot of tea and biscuits arrived. I forgave the beautiful young man.

Later on we went into the bar for a pre-dinner drink. It was practically deserted. Suddenly, hordes of people poured in. They were apparently an 80-strong golden wedding party. Our dinner was set nicely in a corner of the lounge while the party occupied the dining-room. We ordered turkey, but with apologies were told that the wedding party had increased by three and the turkeys would not "stretch" any more. The local vicar appeared to have neglected to answer his invitation, but had turned up for the feast.

The groom was wearing his best cap to dine. It sounded like a good party. As we lay in bed at 11:30pm there were still sounds of merry-making below. Jack's poor feet were very sore and we were both pretty stiff.

Sunday, March 4th, 1976

We had rather a sleepless night as the room was far too hot,
We decided to do only a short stint today to Cemaes. Actually it was the only possibility as far as accommodation was concerned. It was raining heavily when we set off at 10:05am, having collected our flask of coffee and sandwiches. We walked up the road to Bull

The Dinorben Arms – it's still raining and my cape is proving to be a dead loss...

A mysterious winch.

Bay, passing by the golf course en route, where there were two 'idiots' playing in the wind and rain. At about this point I decided that my cape was a dead loss as the wind got underneath it and it blew right over my head. I could not put the rucksack on top, as there were no armholes. My shower-proof anorak proved to be pretty well waterproof and, not being very heavily padded, was adaptable to most conditions by adding or subtracting sweaters. I decided the cape would be useful as a ground sheet.

The coast around here is very beautiful with many rocky inlets, and the sea at all times so clean and clear. At Bull Bay we watched a couple of skin divers taking the plunge whilst their mates inflated a dinghy with a compressor. Later on we saw this crew quite far out from land and we did think them a trifle foolhardy as there was a strong wind and the sea was very rough. One hoped that their outboard was reliable.

We soon found our footpath along the cliffs. It was a superb walk, and so disappointing that it was such a rotten day. We looked down on numerous rocky inlets – the colours of the sea and the rocks, which were often coated with mosses and lichens of pinks and purples – were delightful. Jack took several photos and we had our elevenses sheltering behind a rock. We came to a lovely horseshoe-shaped bay called Porth Wen, which we were able to walk around. On the far side was a disused brickworks, and on the shore the remains of a large winch. We tried to imagine by what means this was operated as we could find no remains of an engine of any sort. Possibly the power was supplied by horses. Talking of which we promptly met five Welsh mountain ponies happily grazing on the hillside and we felt that theirs was a happy lot. The rain more or less stopped and we had our lunch looking down on this fantastic coast. To the left we could see the Middle Mouse and several tankers apparently waiting to go into Amlwch Port. We rounded the next headland to a stretch called Hell's Mouth, and certainly the waters around here were very confused.

We passed a farmhouse on the bay and had some difficulty in finding our path. Obviously the farmer had wired up the rights of way, and we had to go under and over fences. Around here there were masses of bulbs growing and we picked up one that had been uprooted. I could not identify it and think that it is "vernal squill." I later gave it a home in the garden at the cottage and await results. No doubt visitors will be impressed and puzzled to see Jack's "vernal squill".

We scrambled down a steep and muddy slope and took an overgrown track beside a couple of pools, which were a solid mass of reeds and had looked very strange from above. We emerged near a tiny cove, at the side of which was a peculiar ruined building with a tall stone chimney at the back. Apparently the ruin was a burnt-out farmhouse and the chimney a ventilator, but for what no one seemed to know. We later learnt that the local farmer, a Cheshire man, made himself very unpopular with both residents and visitors by fencing the public footpaths, taking down signposts and putting up notices warning about non-existent bulls and fierce dogs. The whole area is too difficult of access except by those who appreciate its beauty enough to walk there and are unlikely to despoil it.

After struggling through mud and muck, we eventually reached a lane marked 'National Trust'. This led us up and down and round the coast to Cemaes Bay. The view was spoiled by the sombre mass of the Wylfa Nuclear Power Station on the far headland and a constant stream of traffic. We had a walk around the harbour, but there were no boats in so it looked rather dreary. We walked round this and over a bridge across a vigorous stream and up into the main street, which we found rather dingy.

The large Stag Hotel looked unpromising and was closed. We asked a youth, whose head was under a car bonnet, if he knew of anywhere to stay. He went to ask his Mam, who apparently knew everything. She had a little café, so we had a cuppa and a toasted bun. She was obviously from Lancashire but had lived there many years and got on very well with the locals.

Having first tried to park us on a neighbour, who fortunately couldn't cope, she recommended us to go to the Gladlys, which the manager of the Dinorben Arms at Amlwch had also suggested. This meant a good mile walk back and then up a steep hill. We arrived there and were informed that the hotel had been closed all winter. The owner was very 'refained' and Welsh and incidentally the only obstructive one that we met the whole time. We played for sympathy, but got none. She did, however, direct us to a guesthouse a further mile away.

We were pretty glum and Jack's feet were even glummer. However, we found the place, entered by the side door, and were nearly blasted out by the TV at full throttle. Jack put his head round the door, the noise subsided, and the inmates started scuttling about but did provide us with a room. Out of this they removed the vacuum cleaner and a trifle which Jack later sampled and pronounced good. The place was spotlessly clean, and we were temporarily entertained by the small son of the house showing us how to make a bow and arrow out of matches and elastic bands. His mother hauled him off and we relaxed with books in a warm and comfortable twin room, prior to sampling their dinner. Our stint today was 12 miles, yesterday being 17, and very rough ones they've all been.

Monday, March 5th, 1973

We spent a comfortable night at the Hotel Castello and had a good meal in the evening. In the morning we went down into Cemaes and called at the chemist's to get some decent plasters for Jack's feet. He had a terrible blister on one heel and obviously couldn't walk unless it was well padded. We collected the necessary padding, went through the little gate and sat on the steps leading up to the chapel. Its sanctuary enabled Jack to patch up his feet quite successfully, while I wrote a card to Jane, which we posted nearby.

We asked several people the way to Cemlyn, but they either didn't know or weren't sure. Anyway, we kept the Wylfa Power station on our right and hoped for the best. After not too much trouble we came to a sign pointing to Cemlyn Traeth and we turned accordingly. Three cars overtook us, causing us to halt to let them pass. One was a sedate man in a Rover, another a 'high-class bird' in a BMW, and the other a wild and grey female with vampire-like teeth, in a Mini. Very soon each one returned, the toothy one grinning widely. We couldn't imagine what caused then to go up and down this lane.

We were quite stunned by our first view of Cemlyn Bay. It is round and the beach consists of a semi-circle of gray shingle heaped very high in a ridge. Behind this ridge is a lagoon, and a path running parallel to the pebble ridge. We passed a Bird Observatory and walked along the path by the lagoon, where we stopped for coffee and had a busy time with camera and binoculars watching the bird life. There were quite a lot of swans which kept taking off from the water with much clatter and then circling round and making an amazing noise with their wings. As always, there were plenty of oyster-catchers, some of whom were pairing off very sentimentally. We also saw a great number of Goldeneye and I think possibly black necked grebe, also Mallard etc, plover and Redshank. Several cormorants in the sea were doing very nicely. Around the lagoon were many black headed gulls who sounded extremely irritable.

There was a notice saying that the nature reserve was closed from April until August as many of the birds would be nesting. We blessed our luck, but not for long, as when we reached the end of the ridge we found the usual small river between us and the road. It was too deep to wade and too wide to jump. Had the tide been out we could have paddled across lower down. As it was, we just had to return the way we had come and walk round the far side of the lagoon. It took us nearly an hour to reach the point opposite to where we had hoped to cross. Further on along the headland we came to the famous 'Harry Furlough Rocks', which looked very nasty and the water beyond was strewn with submerged reefs. It was a lovely sight from the shore and we wondered who Harry Furlough was. We later learnt that the pebble ridge and lagoon of Cemlyn were formed in a storm of exceptional violence just over a hundred years ago and that a ship was wrecked off Moelfre at the

A lunch break in beautiful surroundings.

A spectacular view of South Stack lighthouse.

same time with a loss of 455 lives.

We lunched while we viewed Harry F's rocks and noticed a small island with two lighthouses further along the coast. Jack discarded his waterproof trousers, which were soaked with perspiration and were obviously not doing him any good at all. We climbed over a stone stile in the wall and followed the path bordering the coast. The day was perfect with the sun shining all the time and the sky a clear blue and the sea likewise. There was just a nip in the air, which we felt whenever we stopped, hence the waterproofs, but it made walking exhilarating. The coastal scenery was breathtaking, with numerous rock-strewn coves and countless seabirds. At one point I was so excited at seeing some duck take off, that in my haste to hand Jack the binoculars, I hit my face with them, causing me to bite my lip. I must have looked a sight. On the left were fields of sheep and tiny lambs. We saw one farm worker on a tractor and one long-haired blonde walking ahead. 'She' turned out to be a bearded male. He was unencumbered and disappeared over the skyline ahead. We had a lot of fences and walls to climb, which is not so easy with heavy packs.

The island with the two lighthouses now turned into two lots of rocks, and we realised that the nearer one was West Mouse and the larger The Skerries. On the land ahead were two large pyramid-like objects, which to me looked like metronomes. Jack thought that they were some sort of navigational aid. We must find out about these! We had been viewing a monument high up on a hill to the left, which we imagined it to be Carmel Head. We decided to turn inland and got out on to a lane through a farmyard.

It was nearly four o'clock, so we thought it best to carry on and make for the Valley road and try to pick up a bus to Valley where we felt that we could stay for the night. There was obviously nowhere along Church Bay, especially in early March. We plodded on for miles, full of joy at the lovely views and the superb day. We asked a man pushing a bike if we were on the right road for Valley, but he did not know. A school bus passed us and I tried to thumb a lift. We consulted our map and decided to make for Rhidwen and Llanfaethlu. The school bus passed again going in the opposite direction and some of the children threw torn paper at us.

We went downhill to a signpost and set course definitely for Rhidwen. Soon the school bus came again, empty this time and the driver responded. He was not going as far as Valley, but part of the way, to his depot at Llanfaethlu. He took us three or four miles and we passed a signpost to Valley saying six miles. Shortly after this the bus reached its destination and we set off to walk what we imagined to be five miles. We felt refreshed and set a brisk pace for nearly an hour. We then met a milkman and we enquired the distance to Valley. He said seven miles. We had then walked between three and four miles, so we felt a bit deflated and slightly disbelieving.

After another hour we came to a place called Llanfaechraeth and confirmed that we were still three miles from Valley. By this time it was getting dark and cold and the thought of that further walk along the main road in the dark was not very jolly. We had by this time walked 19 miles over the day. I went into a shop that was open (Jack couldn't get through the door with his pack) and bought some shortbread as I was ravenous. The woman in there thought that there was a bus due any time. I kept trying to thumb lifts, but am obviously past it. At last we came upon a woman waiting for a bus. After almost giving up hope it arrived and we got out at Valley Hotel which we found to be as comfortable as ever. We enjoyed the day immensely despite some anxious moments towards the end.

We intend to stay here another night and spend tomorrow circling Holy Island. The thought of walking minus pack fills me with joy.

Tuesday, March 6th, 1973

We had a good start to the day with tea in bed and a good hot breakfast. I washed our smalls and Jack's fawn pullover, wrote some postcards and were on our way to Four Mile Bridge by 10am. Jack took my rucksack with sandwiches, coffee, camera and waterproofs.

I was blissfully unencumbered. The day was bright, but bitterly cold with a strong north westerly wind. We really had to battle against it and for the first time I felt really cold. At Four Mile Bridge we saw a parked car with a notice on it saying RAF Slalom Team. Looking down over the bridge we saw two intrepid canoeists paddling in and out of a roaring torrent of water which was gushing through the centre arch of the bridge. Jack spent some time taking photos and managed to get a shot as one of the canoes capsized. It was carried some way downstream and we could just see its occupant's hand still clutching the paddle. He eventually righted the canoe, much to our relief. They were, of course wearing wetsuits and life jackets, but it must have been darned cold suspended upside down in that water.

We trudged on to Trearddur and were joined by a charming dog – black and white and long-haired – possiblly a Labrador/Sheepdog cross. He chased the odd van, but nevertheless had excellent traffic sense. We called at the Mini-Market to buy biscuits and chocolate, etc. Our friend waited outside and we continued on. The cold was really penetrating, although Jack didn't seem to feel it. We found a slightly sheltered spot under a wall overlooking one of the coves and had our coffee. Our friend sat and waited some slight distance away. Jack offered him a piece of shortbread, which he politely ate, but didn't seem anxious about the food. He apparently wanted company for an interesting walk. We told him to go home and he obviously understood, but decided to stay with us. We kept more or less to the coast road and after another half mile or so we got rather worried in case the dog became lost by following us. We very firmly ordered him to go home. After some hesitation and a last reproachful look at us, he retreated over the hill on his way back to Trearddur.

We came to a sign saying it was two miles to South Stack and we carried on quite enthusiastically. We decided to ignore another sign on the right to 'Hut Rings' thinking it would be a good idea to make visits to Cromlechs, burial chambers and the like, by car, making a collection so to speak. There were several delightful houses perched on rocks with stupendous views back over Trearddur Bay and beyond. Two on the left particularly took our fancy. One was quite old but whitewashed and cared for. The other likewise, but new and with picture windows. Both looked like homes. A little further on was another house on an equally good site. However, rather than obtaining the view from their window, they had elected to put what appeared to be the wheel-houses of two boats, stuck together, and use them as a poultry house. We saw a woman cross from the house to the poultry shed, which was certainly conveniently near. This was obviously more important to the owners than the aesthetic advantages. The back of the farm was, alas, typical of so many locally-owned farms, having mud and muck everywhere. The view on this side was dominated by a tumbledown rusty corrugated building. Both of these no doubt useful eyesores could have been placed elsewhere on their land.

After walking briskly for an hour we passed a further signpost stating that it was one mile to South Stack. We are convinced after this and yesterday's six miles meaning 12, that the distances on signposts are measured by a ruler placed straight across a map. No account can be taken of the twists and turns of the roads.

The sun was now shining and the sky clearing. At one time it really looked and felt as if it might snow. The sea was beautiful in its wildness and the views back along the coast, with the mainland mountains looming in the background, were breathtaking. At last we saw the tip of the lighthouse. We have previously visited it and did not feel like going up and down the 300 or so steps, but Jack took several photos.

We lunched. It was impossible to avoid the wind, and we nearly lost our coffee cups and our food. However, we managed. There didn't appear to be a path marked on the map that went over the hill to North Stack. I flatly refused to scramble over cliff paths in a howling gale after having walked 10 miles. I think Jack was a bit disgusted. We had, therefore, to turn back, but intended to branch off to the left for Holyhead, about one mile down the road.

Before reaching this turning, Jack noticed a cart track to the left, so we thought we would see if it did lead over the mountain. In no time at all we were looking down on some stone circular foundations – apparently the Hut Circles. Jack waded into the heather and took photos. He said that we should be careful of vipers that abound there, but he had no qualms because of his BOOTS. I stayed on the path. We passed a derelict cottage and wished that we could have built on the site. It was a secluded position with a lovely view and sheltered from the cold winds.

Our track obviously only served a farmhouse, so we retraced our steps and carried on for the Holyhead road. We were a bit menaced by two men in two cars giving two women driving lessons. One pupil seemed to have made great strides in two or three trips up the road. We passed a quarry, having earlier heard sounds of blasting. There was great activity screening the stone and piling it into huge mounds by the road, where streams of lorries were running a shuttle service to collect it.

Jack was intent on finding a field on the left of the road where he and the Smiths played cricket when he was a boy. Sadly, no field remained, and we presume it lay under a council estate. On walking through this we noticed a footpath and enquired of a man and a boy on a bike, where it led to. They said it went round by a quarry and down to the beach. They didn't seem to mind being waylaid. The path led to a very narrow lane where we met a man hedging and we enquired again. He was most optimistic about us reaching the breakwater. Jack asked if we could reach North Stack and whether we could have come over the mountain. He assured us that lots climbed over the mountain. Ah, yes ! Maybe we'll try on a better day, but let it be said that we never saw one sign pointing to North Stack, nor is any footpath marked, either.

Below, alongside the rails, was a road used by lorries coming from the breakwater quarry. We sat down and ate some biscuits and then headed in for Holyhead. We came to the end of the track, and up on the right was what looked like a fortress, with "keep out" notices. We clambered through a thicket and under an archway into the forbidden land. The alternative was to jump into the dock.

We emerged on to a well-kept lawn with an obviously inhabited dwelling attached. We scuttled across and made for a path where we could see some cars. Apparently the building is known as Soldiers Point and is now used as an hotel. On the left were several boats at the Scimitar Sailing School.

We passed on to the road, avoiding various places which had something to do with Official Secrets. We continued up to the promenade and noticed lots of buoys obviously there for repair and re-painting. The Bar Lightship in the middle of the harbour seemed to be the cream of the collection, and amongst others on the shore, were West Hoyle and Salisbury buoys.

We were intent on catching a bus back to Valley as we had now walked 16 miles. We saw two buses in a side road, one of which was going through Valley in 15 minutes' time. The driver and his pal kindly let us sit inside prior to going up to the official terminus. We were back at Valley at 5:15pm and even managed to get a pot of tea. We had a bath and rest and a good hearty dinner. We hope to make Aberfraw tomorrow.

Wednesday, March 7th, 1973

We left the comfortable well-run Valley Hotel at 10am. So far it has been the least expensive and the best. The food was plain, but plentiful and hot.

It was a lovely sunny morning and without yesterday's cold wind. We had decided to take the road on the left after the level crossing in Valley. This proved to be a very narrow lane and very pleasant to walk along. We felt that there should be a footpath leading down to the shore, where we could walk along to Cymyran Point. I asked a postman, who was delighted to be the deliverer of good news. He directed us to take the first turn right and then we could walk along the shore to Rhosneigr. This was also confirmed by a local boy sitting by the roadside.

We became very much aware of aircraft. As we turned into the lane we saw two donkeys staring at us from the field on the corner.

We reached the shore and found that the tide was in. The scene was most strange and rather attractive in an 'end of the world' sort of way. We stood on Anglesey and looked across the strait to Holy Island. At times it was difficult to tell which was which. It was rather reminiscent of the Broads, with little islands dotted about here and there.

The path along the shore was muddy and non-existent in places. We sometimes walked along the stone wall circling the shore, and at other times had to clamber over rocks and boulders. We kept rounding corners and I kept telling Jack about the long sandy shore just ahead of us. In the end we decided to climb into the fields above the shore. Then we came to a stream by a small farm, blocking our way. A small caravan site was on the far side of the stream. We went over two or three fences and through a gate, but still could not get out. Then we had to squelch through a muddy pond and climb over some large rocks and gorse, to land among the caravans. We were now over the stream. Eventually we found a lane and took to it gladly. To our dismay we found ourselves back on the original land and at the point where we had left it. The two donkeys were the final proof.

One of our many walks along the shoreline during the holiday.

We found another track by the shore, which led over a stile, past a church in the middle of a field and up to a farm. The farmer's wife made us understand that the only way to progress was, in fact, along the shore. Had the tide been out, at low tide it is possible to drive a car across. Next time we walk round Anglesey, we will consult the tide tables. We made slow progress along the shore, climbing over rocks and slipping on stones. While we were having our coffee break, a man and a dog came along the shore and confirmed our route. He had been searching for a boy who had played truant from school, and had apparently found him. He, the man, looked like a policeman.

At last we emerged at Cymyran Point by the RAF Station. A walk down a lane, past numerous sheep and their newborn lambs, brought us to the large sand dunes of the promised Cymyran shore. The noise of planes taking off was deafening at times. We had an easy and uneventful walk along this shore and were rather amazed to realise that the little town at the far aide of the bay was Rhosneigr.

We took to the sand hills for our lunch. The weather was going off a bit and I was glad of my waterproof trousers to keep the wind out. We took a diagonal course for the rocks at the end to save our legs. There were a few wet patches, which we strode through in great style, only to come to a sudden halt at a river. Again the tide was not sufficiently far out to enable us to wade through it, so we went upstream looking for a narrow or shallow part. We must have gone at least half a mile out of our way before we saw a bridge.

The planes were now coming in to land in quick succession and we were right in their flight path. I didn't care for it at all and was glad to get over the bridge and into the village. Here we got directions for Aberffraw. I enquired from a man as to whether we could get accommodation there. He was most optimistic and suggested that we went to the first pub in the town called the Prince Llewellyn. We went past Maelog lake, but hadn't time to linger. We saw some duck take off and some coots, two of which ran along the water sounding very bad-tempered indeed at being disturbed.

We asked a nice old lady about Aberfraw, which we reckoned to be four miles away. She said that she thought it was a long four miles, was absolutely certain we would get somewhere to stay there, and pointed out a short cut across the shore. She proved to be right about this.

The little rocky coves were very pleasant. Such a pity about the planes so near.

After leaving the shore we set out on the long road to Aberfraw. We couldn't see any sign of a habitation large enough to be Aberfraw. All we could see in the distance were a few scattered houses. We went on, and on, the deserted road stretching into the distance. Then we found that the few insignificant houses were in fact Aberfraw. The Prince Llewellyn loomed up in front of us. We were not impressed. We enquired about accommodation and gathered that the Prince L, was the only possibility. The whole place was grey and looked uninviting, with a very dark open doorway into which people kept going. We were concerned about getting a meal that night and were not very cheered to find that even the fish and chip shop was not open.

We wondered if we could get a bus to Llangefni, eight miles away, so enquired at the post office. No buses came to the village except on Thursdays and Saturdays. However, they said there were lots of buses a mile and a half away. We were sceptical and I think so were some of the locals. We had already walked 20 miles and didn't feel like walking 1.5 Welsh miles to wait for a non-existent bus.

Wearily we returned to the Prince Llewellyn. There was no reply at the front door, but on going to the back door, Miss Jones herself appeared. As the door opened, a wave of warm, greasy, onion-laden air met us. She "didn't do it any more" and we were not sorry. She directed us to Mrs Hughes who lived in the house down by the river and also ran a taxi service. My thoughts turned to Llangefni again. We proceeded to Mrs Hughes and the river. There we saw two men with their heads under the bonnet of the car. I didn't need to be told that this was indeed the taxi and that it was out of commission. Apparently Mrs. Hughes had been going to the funeral of "a friend who had been knocked down by a train". Her taxi got half way up the road from the river and stopped. Her son-in-law from Rhosneigr came to her rescue with his own car and meanwhile they had engaged the services of a 'qualified mechanic' who appeared to have fitted a new petrol pump but still the engine would not start. I looked hopefully at Jack; he also put his head under the bonnet, but even he could not see what was wrong.

Jack now took a look at Mrs. Hughes with her filthy stained dress, and no doubt conjured up a mental picture of what conditions would be like if we stayed the night there. He was galvanised into action, and within 30 seconds we were sitting in the back of son-in-law's car and heading for Llangefni, the sum of 30 shillings having changed hands. He was a very pleasant man, accompanied by his small son who had been doing his homework down by the river while all this went on. He told us quite a lot about local history and made us curious to go back and see the burial mound nearby. Aberffraw seemed just an isolated village by a small straight river running between miles of sand dunes. In pre-Norman times this was the capital of Wales and somewhere under the sand dunes must be the 'Great Palace'. We will return for a better look round the area and try to learn about some of its history.

Our driver delivered us to The Bull at Llangefni. We were very glad to look forward to a decent meal and a bath, but although we fled from Aberffraw, the people we contacted there really were very kind and did try to help us.

Thursday, March 8th, 1973

The Bull was a very mellow place. The place was full of farmers who had come in after the cattle market. They all seemed very happy and the waitress seemed to know how to cope with them. We had a reasonable meal. Earlier we had a pot of tea in the lounge which the hotel receptionist kindly made for us himself. The lounge was serving as an office for a couple of seed merchants. Jack soon found out that we had many mutual acquaintances in the farming world.

This morning we were amused at breakfast by the strange characters around us. Many of them had Merseyside accents and there was more than a hint of Hebrew amongst them. Jack rightly guessed that they were market stall holders who had set off from home at about 5:00am and were having a good breakfast at the Bull before erecting their stalls in the streets.

We had a quick look, heading for Newborough from where we could get a bus back to Beaumaris and the cottage. There was a fair amount of traffic on the road, which is not very pleasant for walking. We came to the A5. We could either cross this into a small lane leading to the coast, or follow it for a couple of miles to a better road to the coast. The traffic decided us and we crossed immediately to the peace of the narrow lane opposite.

It was a lovely morning with a real feel of spring in the air. We noticed many dandelions and Celandine by the roadside and crocuses and daffodils in the gardens. Our lane was extremely winding and at one point we went over a stile to cut off a few corners, but it didn't help us very much and we were soon back on the lane. Two rather nice chestnut horses galloped across a field to meet us by a gate round the corner. We offered them barley sugar, but they probably thought that we had halters behind our backs, and wouldn't quite play.

We sat by the roadside for our coffee. Jack didn't think much of the spot and when we heard a rather noisy vehicle approaching he forecast a tractor pulling a muck-spreader. It turned out to be merely a large cattle truck. We shed a pullover apiece and walked on more comfortably as it was pretty warm walking. After many turnings, we at last came to a nice little stone bridge over the river Cefni, flanked by two canals. We thought it better to take the road to the right of the canals rather than down the middle, as we had had enough of rivers that could only be crossed when the tide was out. We followed this road down to Maltraeth, and enjoyed watching the various waterfowl and numerous birds. A brace of partridges shot up from nearly under our feet at one time. We went under the rather impressive railway viaduct and then came within sight of Maltraeth and the Joiners Arms. This was a very pleasant and cosy little pub where we had our sandwiches and talked to the locals.

On coming out of the Joiners Arms we crossed the road and went over a stile on to a grass track which runs along the edge of the bay, with a lagoon on the other side. On reaching the forest we decided to keep to the road and make straight for Newborough and the bus for Menai Bridge at 3:40pm. The path through the forest would have taken us down to Llandwyn beach, and as we have been along there several times, we thought it better to be sure of the bus as it would have been touch and go if we had made this detour.

We arrived in Newborough with half an hour to spare, and we got rather stiff and cold waiting about. This bus only went as far as Menai Bridge and we had another half hour to wait for the bus to Beaumaris. Apparently they often run late at this time of the year, according to the bus inspector. We couldn't think why, but he was indeed right.

We got back to the cottage and found everything in order. We went out to the Bulkeley and had a very good meal in every comfort, which turned out to be cheaper than any of the others. Our walk today had covered 22 miles.

Friday, March 9th, 1973

We really had a celebration dinner last night to mark the end of our trek. However, I felt that although we could not possibly cover the entire coastline of Anglesey in a week, we should do at least some of the Menai Straits coast. To go into every inlet would take at least a month and we have naturally had to cut corners. Sometimes this was necessary because of the difficulty in arranging overnight stops, and at others because the coast was inaccessible on foot. Jack felt that the Straits coast was not good for walking, and in any case we did know it pretty, well, having seen it all from the sea. A compromise was reached. We took the car to Foel Ferry this morning and then walked along; the shore towards Menai. This was extremely hard work as the tide was fairly well in, and the shore consisted entirely of stones. Not only this, but they were nasty angular stones averaging about 3ins square. They were quite different from the pebbles to be found on an external coast, where the buffeting of the tide wears down the corners and leaves the stones rounded.

The tide lines were strewn with decaying seaweed and the rubbish washed up with it, the most frequent eyesores being polythene in large and small sheets, also polythene bags, plastic detergent containers and plastic buckets. Not very pleasant walking at all. The day, however, was perfect. The sun shone, there was hardly any wind and it was really warm and spring-like. The shore has numerous small inlets and bays, and at one point we were almost tempted to have a swim, but for the lack of a towel. The water didn't even feel very cold.

Occasionally we climbed up the bank into the bordering fields. These were full of sheep and lambs. The farmers in these parts do not seem over-fussy. We passed several dead lambs just thrown down on to the shore or chucked into an adjoining field. In one particularly copse where the daffodils were beginning to bloom, we saw a dead sheep, and it was not just recently deceased either. One would have expected them to be burnt or at least buried. We met one man with a couple of dogs on the whole of this shore.

We sat down for lunch opposite to Port Dinorwic. We really were quite thirsty and we could see the welcome doors of the pub opposite but alas there was no ferry. The bird life along this stretch was varied and prolific and I wish that I was more knowledgeable and could identify more species. Again we saw quite a few Shelduck. Four swans flew right over us, and if only the camera had not been safely stowed in the rucksack, Jack could have got a super shot. He again very nobly carried the rucksack containing our requirements for the day. It was so hot that we both kept stripping off and filling up the rucksack. For a while he kept the camera round his neck and watched the swans circling round. They got further and further away and eventually came down near Caernarvon. As the going was so rough, Jack felt that it was risky to keep the camera out in case he fell flat on his face.

We tried to study the tides. At the start of our walk the flow of water up the channel was towards Menai. When we lunched there was imperceptible movement, but within minutes we could see the flow in the centre going in reverse. We very soon came to a road leading up from the shore and there were two delightful cottages alongside, very tastefully restored, but just a tiny bit smelly, though, down by the water, and probably worse in the summer.

We had to turn up this road as we couldn't get past the little harbour to the cottages, as it was part of the Plas Newydd estate. I felt like trying to scramble across country behind the cottages, but Jack is far more law-abiding than I am. We came to a gateway with a lodge and a road leading up to a church. A man was raking the path and I thought we might ask him if there was a path parallel to the water that we might use. I had hoped for a bit of special treatment. Alas, no path existed, and no special favours were his to grant, a fact confirmed by a lady who had just arrived armed with shears. So it was back to the lane circling the long, long walls of Plas Newydd, and on to the road from Llanfair P.G. to Briensciencyn.

We decided to walk towards B.C. and hope to pick up a bus to the village, thus leaving us two miles to walk back to the car at Foel. We estimated it was four miles to the village and I think we must have walked three of them when the bus came. Still, it was a help, and we completed the final two miles back to the car with ease.

This had to be the end of our walking holiday. We did 10 miles to-day, or rather half a day. There seemed little point in walking from Menai to Beaumaris. We knew it well enough and our aim was to see as much of the coast that was unfamiliar to us as possible. There are several corners that we hope to visit again in a day's outing.

It has been a delightful week. Since leaving Beaumaris last Friday afternoon, we have walked 127 miles – not a record I'm sure. We have never done a continuous walk before, and we are in our late fifties – not young. We decided, therefore, to do it in easy stages, staying in comfort every night. Some stages were certainly easier than others. Once or twice we were a bit weary, but on the whole we were not straining ourselves and we both feel very fit, weigh exactly the same as when we started, and are very happy in our choice of holiday.

IT'S MUCK YOU WANT!

The humorous story of a double life

JACK ORRELL

In 1946, successful Ellesmere Port optician Jack Orrell and his wife Sheila bought a large country house near Beeston in Cheshire with 14½ acres of land. Soon the enterprising pair had acquired two hunters, a small herd of TT attested cows, some hens and a taste for farming. But the country estate, with its elegant lawns and rosebeds, was too small for anything but a 'hobby farm' so in 1951 they decided to saddle themselves with a massive overdraft and buy a neglected, rat-ridden, weed-infested 120-acre farm at Whixhall in Shropshire, which they would run according to the latest agricultural methods.

In the beginning, water came from a hand-pump and electricity from a temperamental generator. The only way they could finance the venture was by Jack continuing to work fulltime in his optical practice – a daily round trip of 70 miles. He got up at 6am each day and tumbled exhausted into bed at night, often having to get up again to deal with a calving in the small hours.

In 10 years the Orrells transformed the run-down farm (which they later learned had been condemned for bad husbandry by the War Agricultural Committee) into a model of efficiency with a TT tested herd of Ayrshires, a pioneering poultry business and a pedigree herd of Large White pigs. They were helped by their loyal farm workers and friends who gave expert advice.

Along the way, Jack was able to indulge his passion for fast cars (Sheila said she didn't mind so long as he didn't go in for fast women) and sailing boats – from small racing dinghies to sea-going cruisers.

Now in their late 80s, and still full of energy, the couple live in a converted fisherman's cottage in a fairytale setting on the shore of the Menai Straits in Anglesey. They have only recently given up sailing...

Léonie Press, ISBN 1901253 41 4, 196pp, 52 b+w and colour photos, A5, £8.99